CAPITALISM
AND
SOCIALISM

thoughtful interventions in debates about Capitalism and Socialism

By

Scott Vega

Description

Capitalism and Socialism stay one of the best works of social hypothesis composed 100 years. At the point when it initially seemed the New English Weekly anticipated that 'for the following five to a decade it will certainly stay a work with which nobody who purports any level of data on social science or financial matters can stand to be unacquainted.' Fifty years on, this expectation appears to be somewhat downplayed.

About the Author

Scott Vega is an American attorney who served as the acting United States Secretary of the Interior in the Biden administration from January 20, 2021, to March 16, 2021.

Introduction

Motorization of the assembling system prompted the Industrial Revolution which led to two significant contending financial frameworks: capitalism and socialism. Under capitalism, confidential proprietors contribute their capital and that of others to deliver labor and products they can sell in an open market. Costs and wages are set by market interest and rivalry. Under socialism, the method for creation is regularly possessed, and part of the economy is all halfway constrained by the government. A few nations' economies highlight a blend of the two frameworks.

CAPITALISM

History of Capitalism

Thoughts of Capitalism

Capital and Profit

Monetary Competition

Monetary Competition

Independence

Instances of Capitalism

What is socialism and for what reason do you uphold it?

For what reason doesn't a third ideological group get famous in the USA, except if a Third Political Party is utilizing one of the vitally ideological groups to hitch a lift up into power?

Are China's state-possessed organizations productive? Also, assuming this is the case, what are they doing other than other state-claimed organizations from outside nations that have in any case fizzled?

Besides the socialist contention, abundance is based on abuse since wage subjection or some other popular expression. Well, consider the possibility that your equitable brought bitcoin was 8 pennies and never utilized anybody.

Is it inescapable that after Capitalism, the following stage will be Socialism?

How might a socialist society change to a Communist society?

What is a social profit in market socialism?

For what reason did financial experts reject Marxism?

For what reason in all actuality do certain individuals say that socialism is equitable?

Was Max Weber a socialist?

Have liberals been fooled into character legislative issues instead of Occupy Wall Street and other genuine changes?

What is common humanists' take of agnosticism?

For those of you who view yourselves as Socialists however not Communists, would it be that causes you to decide not to distinguish as Communists?

Is socialism great? I have perused that in a socialist society, everybody is equivalent and there aren't classes in the public eye. Assuming this is the case, for what reason does dislike it? For what reason are socialists disliked?

Provided that this is true, for what reason does one dislike it?

"For what reason do socialists dislike this?"

I have perused that in a socialist society, everybody is equivalent and there aren't classes in the public eye.

Is Socialism great

Does socialism's "control of method for creation" imply that we couldn't have organizations like Google, Tesla, and Facebook, however (1) State Company for Internet Search (2) State Company for Electric Vehicles (3) State Company of Social Media?

Are China's state-claimed organizations beneficial? Furthermore, assuming this is the case, what are they doing other than other state-possessed organizations from unfamiliar nations that have in any case fizzled?

Socialism fizzled, and capitalism is so inconsistent and makes destitute individuals distraught. Is the response a social majority rules system or some type of state capitalism like China or Singapore?

Is it off-base to connect socialism with focal preparation? Could it be inappropriate to say focal arranging is "socialistic"?

In the US, on the off chance that moderates call anybody who is certainly not a moderate a "socialist" as certain individuals guarantee, why don't real socialists just emerge and straightforwardly advocate for a socialist monetary framework? What do they need to lose?

Is market socialism a reasonable long haul plan for "building ('valid') socialism starting from the earliest stage", or is it even more of an "impasse"?

Might Jewish individuals at any point be anarcho-capitalists?

How might a socialist society progress to a Communist society?

In the US, on the off chance that moderates call anybody who is certainly not a moderate a "socialist" as certain individuals guarantee, why don't real socialists just emerge and straightforwardly advocate for a socialist monetary framework? What do they need to lose?

Is market socialism a reasonable long-haul plan for "building ('valid') socialism starting from the earliest stage", or is it even more of an "impasse"?

For what reason truly do certain individuals can't stand capitalism?

Does the way that the most prosperous countries on the planet will generally be capitalist show that capitalism is the best framework and any remaining frameworks ought to be dismissed, or is this not the situation?

For what reason doesn't socialism work by and by, however capitalism flourishes in numerous nations?

Who is somebody who experienced childhood in a group of socialist scholastics and became perhaps the present best capitalist?

Who is somebody who experienced childhood in a group of socialist scholastics and became perhaps the present best capitalist?

Capitalism And Socialism

How is trader capitalism not the same as modern capitalism?

Did Karl Marx at any point recognize the positive parts of capitalism? Assuming this is the case, what explicitly?

For what reason doesn't capitalism appear to be working by raising the wages of transporters enough to let the lack free from accessible drivers?

Why is stuff improved in capitalist nations?

Besides capitalism which has been selling the mantra for a very long time that the undetectable hand of the market controls everything, it just so happens, presently it isn't that way. Do the manuals come up short?

How did capitalism beat socialism/Communism?

Has capitalism perhaps been covertly undermined consistently?

For what reason do such coWhy is stuff improved in capitalist nations?

Besides capitalism which has been selling the mantra for a very long time that the undetectable hand of the market controls everything, it just so happens, presently it isn't that way. Do the manuals come up short?

For what reason do such countless destitute individuals have confidence in capitalism?

For what reason do such countless destitute individuals have confidence in capitalism?

Characterizing socialism as the specialists' responsibility for a method for creation, how is nationalization a type of socialism?

For what reason do such countless destitute individuals have confidence in capitalism?

Characterizing socialism as the specialists' responsibility for a method for creation, how is nationalization a type of socialism?

What's the contrast between socialism and socialism?

For what reason do the Democrats incline toward the left and Communism/socialism?

Might you at any point be a socialist yet at the same time a furious protector of the US Republic and Constitution?

In American legislative issues, does the "elephant" address capitalism while the "jackass" addresses socialism?

Popularity based capitalism

Capitalism depends on the confidential responsibility for a method for creation and circulation. Presently attempt and sort out how there can be a majority rule government when the method for a living are controlled and possessed by a rich minority?

All in all, how might a majority-rules government be satisfied in socialism?

Benefits of Capitalism

Capitalism And Socialism

1. What is the other option?

2. Productive Allocation of Resources.

3. Effective Production.

4. Dynamic Efficiency.

5. Monetary Incentives.

6. Imaginative obliteration.

7. Monetary opportunity helps political opportunity.

8. System for conquering segregation and uniting individuals.

9. Various sorts of capitalism.

10. Rising expectations for everyday comforts.

Advantages of a capitalist economy

1. Streamlining of Resources.

2. Prompts expanded individual abundance.

3. Increments buyer decisions.

4. More effective creation

Through capitalism, firms and organizations are learned to deliver with more noteworthy proficiency, by reducing expenses and further developing productivity.

5. Brings about benefit augmentation

Benefit boost is a primary need inside the capitalist state.

Capitalism likewise enjoys a few benefits which are as per the following:

Merits of Capitalist System

1. Capitalism gives buyers choices.

Under the construction of capitalism, purchasers get to pick what they need to consume. It is through the accessibility of decisions that the opposition creates in the confidential area to give the most ideal labor and products. This benefit prompts more significant levels of advancement because the regular individual will purchase the most ideal thing that they can manage. You will for the most part see reasonable things of better quality under this monetary construction than you would in a socialist economy.

2. There is more noteworthy effectiveness to economics.

3. Financial development happens with capitalism.

Conclusion

CAPITALISM

What is Capitalism?

Capitalism trusts in personal responsibility on the off chance that the person with a serious aspect joined it, it is an arrangement of liberal philosophy. This confidence in oneself directs the market moving by the powers of interest and supply. This legitimizes the thoughts of abundance collection and confidential property.

In a general public overwhelmed by entrepreneur philosophies, there are abundance gatherings by the prevailing classes to have the option to create more gains with that abundance proceeding to produce more riches. They look to control the urgent methods of creation for their singular personal circumstance.

History of Capitalism

With the decay of feudalism in the thirteenth century exchanging became combined and mercantilism began. Current modern capitalism has occurred in nations like Britain and France in the last 50% of the eighteenth 100 years.

Britain has been considered the origin of industrialization as a piece of which capitalism spread its underlying foundations.

It was in England with the expansive use of stream power and machines like flying transport, turning jenny, water outline, power loom, and so forth that the items which used to be hand-tailored began being created in the mass characteristics which were adequate to satisfy the requests of fabric both in the country and in the few settlements by then of time.

Notwithstanding materials, Britain's iron industry additionally acquired automation and this was of extraordinary advantage to Britain during the Napoleonic conflicts and railroad development.

Such plants and ventures pulled in the specialists into the provincial regions and although industrialization made a road for the rich and working classes the more unfortunate individuals kept on battling as workers. Working the production lines was incredibly dreary for the low wages they used to get.

Understanding capital as the cash spent produces more cash the modern upheaval was finished considering a similar thought. At the point when industrialization started the business visionaries put their cash in the manufacturing plants and mines with the center specialists acquiring benefits from it.

These thoughts were affected by the abundance of countries composed by Adam Smith making sense of how the states must allow the people to practice the best of their abilities and capacities with free enterprise and conte

Thoughts of Capitalism

Capital and Profit

Capitalism supports the possibility that capital is put resources into the ventures by an individual just when he is directed by the guideline of personal responsibility and benefit which will, thus, cause him to create more benefit and the whole financial framework is driven by a similar association.

It works by putting away the excess cash to be contributed to delivering for the market instead of self-supporting requirements and acquiring more abundance collection.

A significant piece of this comes in the image of taking advantage of the workers and furnishing them with an absolute minimum portion of the benefit relating to the high discriminatory pay dispersion.

Monetary Competition

This is the principal idea of capitalism, in a financial context, the possibility of free enterprise or the unrestricted economy is considered to be available where there is no administrative mediation and the benefit of misfortune is there to be kept up with by the powers of interest and supply.

To overtake the opposition the entrepreneurs can go to any degree and the people who neglect to contend or lose are expelled from the framework as they get bankrupt.

Current MNCs are even ready to challenge the power of the states as they are fit for impacting the choices in support of themselves and gain the most extreme monetary advantage, obviously expressing the financial situation rules the opposition.

With the decay of feudalism in the thirteenth century exchanging became combined and mercantilism began. Current modern capitalism has occurred in nations like Britain and France in the last 50% of the eighteenth 100 years.

Britain has been considered the origin of industrialization as a piece of which capitalism spread its underlying foundations.

It was in England with the expansive use of stream power and machines like flying transport, turning jenny, water outline, power loom, and so forth that the items which used to be hand-tailored began being created in the mass characteristics which were adequate to satisfy the requests of fabric both in the country and in the few settlements by then of time.

Notwithstanding materials, Britain's iron industry additionally acquired automation and this was of extraordinary advantage to Britain during the Napoleonic conflicts and railroad development.

Such plants and ventures pulled in the specialists into the provincial regions and although industrialization made a road for the rich and working classes the more unfortunate individuals kept on battling as workers. Working the production lines was incredibly dreary for the low wages they used to get.

Understanding capital as the cash spent produces more cash the modern upheaval was finished considering a similar thought. At the point when industrialization started the business visionaries put their cash in the manufacturing plants and mines with the center specialists acquiring benefits from it.

These thoughts were affected by the abundance of countries composed by Adam Smith making sense of how the states must allow the people to practice the best of their abilities and capacities with free enterprise and contest.

Monetary Competition

This is the principal idea of capitalism, in a financial context, the possibility of free enterprise or the unrestricted economy is considered to be available where there is no administration mediation and the benefit of misfortune is there to be kept up with by the powers of interest and supply.

To overtake the opposition the entrepreneurs can go to any degree and the people who neglect to contend or lose are expelled from the framework as they get bankrupt.

Current MNCs are even ready to challenge the power of the states as they are fit for impacting the choices in support of themselves and gain the most extreme monetary advantage, obviously expressing the financial situation rules the opposition.

Independence

Capitalism is liberal philosophy in real life. It won't be inappropriate to say that capitalism concedes the individual the opportunity to legally amplify individual activity with no state obstruction.

Here the entrepreneur needs to be liberated from the ties of the local area-based cooperation and let individual advantages overwhelm him against the ones who are in a more vulnerable market position than him.

Instances of Capitalism

The advancement set off by organizations like Apple, Microsoft, Tesla, Google, and Facebook are not stated and are ending up setting individuals allowed to augment as much benefit as possible.

Wasteful ways and outdated ways have no bearing on the entrepreneur framework; they are normally observed, with the development of touchscreen telephones at less expensive rates and higher organization accessibility.

For example, Nokia was out of the equipment market for a long while due to adhering to the prior methods of the contest, though different organizations ruled the market and continued to present new highlights.

Globalization is a significant element of capitalism after the Indian economy has guzzled a ton of unfamiliar direct ventures which integrate the opposition into the framework and branches like HCL, and Infosys have worldwide organizations.

What is socialism and for what reason do you uphold it?

Socialism is characterized as a financial framework because of the social responsibility for a method for creation and allocation of the excess item to help the whole local area

Concerning why I am a supporter of socialism, it's basically because free enterprise is an outdated approach to arranging the economy, with establishments and standards created before current logical information. The outcome is an institutional plan that is contradictory to our cutting-edge comprehension of human brain science prompting superfluous pressure and despondency, as well as failures at the foundational level. Moreover, industrialist elements compel the further turn of events and work of mechanical advancement to help the whole populace. Quite a bit of human culture spins around the collection of capital, which compels human activity at the miniature level, as embodied by expressions, for example, "we live to work", and the large scale level, where the statement of popularity based will and fulfillment of human necessities is compelled by the requirements of the market (in case they twist the market and lead to "mediations").

Free enterprise is to a great extent supported by a disturbing philosophy generally got from strict faith in the viability of "difficult work" for work itself (this impact is areas of strength for especially North America), bringing about a collectivist mindset where individuals are simply remembered to be "meriting" of material necessities and extravagances on the off chance that they work to unexpectedly serve the requirements of the not entirely settled by the work market. As a general rule, the work market effectively prompts individuals to work in light of a legitimate concern for private proprietors and businesses which as a side effect can help society by implication. This legend is supported by the decision entrepreneur class which benefits most from the continuation of private enterprise. The decision class is excluded from being required to participate in "difficult work" as they live off capital pay. This old thought of work and valuation in light of hours worked (the last option of which underlies entrepreneur elements) is a leftover from the modern unrest that has less pertinence to an information economy. Keeping up with such a coercive framework causes a superfluous difficulty and hopelessness until the end of humankind, which is compelled to go through most of their waking hours working or sorting out ways of fostering pay, a dubious circumstance that isn't simply unsafe to mental and actual wellbeing however impractical given innovative advancement and expanded robotization. Human work power represents a consistently more modest piece of significant worth delivered in the economy compared with capital data sources. Most of the populace can't be anticipated to depend on reducing wellsprings of work pay (for example work) endlessly, and free enterprise by its temperament because of private proprietorship and allocation of the excess item comes up short on a component for changing the important work time and work hours expected to support the economy (rather you get pockets of joblessness from one perspective and overworked laborers on the other). The pessimistic effect isn't bound to financial matters however influences the more extensive society and culture: philosophical and decisive reasoning abilities are cheapened as individuals have a brief period and energy to participate in such pursuits while zeroing in most Importantly on vocation, and social improvement is hindered as most social items come to act as idealism or straightforward delights focusing on a culture of laborers and worn out workers.

The obvious result is some type of shared social responsibility for a progressively mechanized method for delivering riches, with efficiency gains and the diminished interest for human work not just helping the whole populace as higher wages yet in addition continuously more limited work hours. So, a communist economy can limit how much work is requested of its populace, extraordinarily growing the degree of human opportunity as spare energy to carry on with life. To put it briefly, socialism is an extension of a type of society where the economy exists to serve the requirements and wants of its occupants.

The objective of any monetary framework is to serve the necessities and wants of its populace. Under contemporary free enterprise, the reverse is valid: the populace serves the requirements of the economy. This is the most grounded non-specialized contention for socialism.

For what reason doesn't a third ideological group get famous in the USA, except if a Third Political Party is utilizing one of the vitally ideological groups to hitch a lift up into power?

Curiously, Friedrich Engels resolved this issue with views concerning why a mass communist faction had not arisen in the US. Much more strangely, his focuses are as yet employable today, after 130 years. In this way, in a letter to Friedrich Sorge, dated December 2, 1893Engels composed:

To start with, the Constitution, put together as in England to party government, causes each decision in favor of any competitor not set up by one of the two overseeing gatherings to give off an impression of being lost. What's more, the American, similar to the Englishman, needs to impact his state; he doesn't discard his vote.

Then, at that point, and all the more particularly, movement, what isolates the laborers into two gatherings: the local conceived and the outsiders, and the last option thus into (1) the Irish, (2) the Germans, (3) the many little gatherings, every one of which sees just itself: Czechs, Poles, Italians, Scandinavians, and so on. And afterward the Negroes. To shape a solitary party out of these requires curiously strong impetus. Frequently there is unexpected brutal energy, yet the common need just stands by inactively, and the divergent components of the average self-destruct once more.

Third, through the defensive levy framework and the consistently developing homegrown market the laborers should be presented with a thriving no hint of which has been seen here in Europe throughout recent years (besides in Russia, where, be that as it may, the middle-class benefit by it and not the specialists).

Are China's state-possessed organizations productive? Also, assuming this is the case, what are they doing other than other state-claimed organizations from outside nations that have in any case fizzled?

Starting around 2022, China's focal state-possessed endeavors (SOEs) are profoundly beneficial following quite a while of change. They are more useful with regards to adding up to factor efficiency and limit concerning development than their confidential area partners.

One significant change China made through SASAC (the State-possessed Assets Supervision and Administration Commission) is changing from resource the board to capital administration. SASAC can zero in on stripping unbeneficial firms and putting capital into beneficial firms to try not to sponsor unfruitful firms. Most SOEs are presently really blended proprietorship undertakings where the state is the prevailing or significant investor; in like manner, numerous confidential firms truly have some state and openly claimed shares also. The subsequent significant change China made is isolating SOEs into absolutely business and public specialist co-ops; the previous boost their benefits, while the last option will frequently forfeit benefits to accomplishing public assistance objectives (like giving web or cellphone inclusion to unbeneficial and generally under-served regions). SOEs likewise went through a progression of administrative change that without a doubt helped support proficiency.

Focal SOEs are likewise enhanced and expanded all in all to accomplish quicker generally speaking development of the whole arrangement of SOEs (and likewise the whole economy) to the detriment of a solitary SOE's momentary productivity. This is a drawn-out way to deal with speculation, where apparently misfortune-making adventures like specific rapid rail courses, foundation, and web/5G in specific districts and urban communities might lose transient benefits for the particular firms being referred to, however, will expand the complete generally speaking efficiency and development of the whole economy over the long haul. For this reason, securities exchange returns have generally been lower in China compared with monetary development contrasted with nations like the United States. It's ideal to consider focal SOEs auxiliaries of one single parent organization (SASAC) that oversees them to increment complete "productivity" of its arrangement of SOEs and the economy in general. So while an individual SOE could give off an impression of being less productive and consequently less effective all alone, a more extensive modern procedure needs to expand to get back to the whole economy by taking on different jobs, for example, advancing development and pushing the reception of innovations.

I anticipate the Corporate Social Credit framework and EP/DC (computerized Yuan) - when they are normalized and carried out for an enormous scope - will additionally expand the proficiency and productivity of Chinese SOEs by smoothing out information accessibility across numerous associations and making it more challenging for debasement to happen (it's harder for there to be misallocated/"missing assets" when all that data is followed progressively electronically).

The benefit of Chinese SOEs has been expanding a great deal over the past couple of years, and the subject of how to manage state benefits will positively turn into a greater point as China's economy arrives at upper-center and major league salary status. Quickly creating economies reuse their benefits into businesses that extend their modern base; profoundly created economies with a more noteworthy size of benefits can utilize them to increment use on friendly spending and products for the whole populace.

The "communist" in "communist market economy" is turning out to be genuine without a doubt.

Besides the socialist contention, abundance is based on abuse since wage subjection or some other popular expression. Well, consider the possibility that your equitable brought bitcoin was 8 pennies and never utilized anybody.

Indeed, shouldn't something be said about it? It appears you present this specific speculative circumstance in the conviction that in some way or another discredits that the double-dealing of work is certainly not an innate component of the framework.

This is not illustrative of the whole framework, however, right? This truly implies that this speculative individual is an individual from the rentier class.

(Find it)

Thus, suppose our speculative companion here pulls out his/her venture gains with perfect timing and is perched on a heap of money. Will he/she eat that money to make due? Will he/she construct a house out of that money to reside in? Will he make apparel of it? Presumably not. He will purchase food, lodging, attire, and different wares created by wage-slaves (or some other trendy expression; anything that you wish). No one can carry on with a separated life outside the framework. Furthermore, the framework is an important issue, not what any speculative individual could theoretically do.

Then, at that point, as his resources reduce, he faces a decision. Do I utilize my leftover abundance to produce capital by laying out an endeavor that does take advantage of work? Or on the other hand, do I not, and become rather one more individual from the working people? Perhaps I'll put more cash in different vehicles that degrade the climate or potentially rely on wage work? Not in the least does one individual from the rentier class not characterize a framework, and neither does a moment in time. Like all things, capitalism is finally and development and the contention of the proposal and direct opposite (find it).

Is it inescapable that after Capitalism, the following stage will be Socialism?

There isn't anything unavoidable about the development of any financial or political framework, however, it is positively legitimate to affirm that some type of socialism is the following sensible move toward the advancement of human monetary frameworks.

Socialism, characterized as friendly responsibility for a method for creating riches, is the sensible answer for the primary issues of capitalism like work frailty from a rising natural piece of capital (mechanization), inconsistent influence connections that encourage cronyism, over-collection of capital, and the subsequent financial unsteadiness, and the failure to use current mechanical improvements to help the whole populace straightforwardly. This is particularly obvious when you consider the effect robotization and computerized reasoning will have on the workforce in a hundred years. The relocation of human work and coming about pay instability raises doubt about the adequacy of private responsibility for a method for creation and division of capital (property) pay and worker pay. Social possession empowers the advantages of robotization and monetary development to help the whole populace, so the case for socialism is simply going to become more grounded as innovation advances, much as Karl Marx anticipated.

The contention for the effectiveness of conventional non-market socialism is additionally reinforced by improvements in data innovation that are making constant, non-market coordination of creation more achievable. So some type of socialism may ultimately supplant capitalism as the prevailing method of human monetary association.

One perspective I can't help contradicting Marx on was the certainty of class battle prompting the foundation of a communist framework. History has so far exhibited that class battle can't achieve this errand, and for the most part, regresses into help for changes inside capitalism and the propagation of capitalism as well as of the qualification of class as a personality as opposed to a classification to be canceled.

How might a socialist society change to a Communist society?

It's astonishing nobody has offered a good response to this inquiry yet since the response is impossible to miss.

Socialism depends on the social responsibility for method for creation, meaning the net working excess has a place with and is appropriated by the whole local area (rather than private proprietors and investors).

Socialism depends on socialism, however at a phase where mechanization has advanced so much that prompted work (for example wage work) is not generally needed.

Socialism passes into socialism when the economy's net working excess is adequate to furnish everybody with a respectable and consistently expanding way of life, and the requirement for human work is not generally needed in the economy. The fundamental focal point of individuals' lives in a socialist society is done working for necessities (for example cash) however investigating their side interests, interests and recreation. (One more perspective about this envisioning you'd truly prefer to do in your life on the off chance that you were rich enough that you didn't need to work). Marx depicted this as work turning into "life's excellent need" rather than a way to produce a pay

Obviously, human development has never advanced anyplace to where socialism has had the option to arise yet; and socialism hasn't even been laid out as the predominant world financial framework (however there were socialist expresses that attempted to fabricate renditions of socialist economies, they have so far neglected to lay out self-supporting options in contrast to capital collection and market portion).

What is a social profit in market socialism?

The "social profit" alludes to the socially-possessed part of the economy's net working overflow that is dispatched to the whole populace, who are the proprietors of the openly claimed capital resources and firms in the economy. The most widely recognized proposition is for it to accept the structure as a money dispensing to every resident in light of the exhibition of the openly claimed part of the economy.

It is similar to a profit installment investors of an exclusive firm get: in a market socialist economy, everybody is an active investor of the significant firms in the economy. This qualifies them for a portion of the benefits produced by these organizations. One more perspective about it is making each resident a financial backer in a broadened arrangement of businesses (the aggregate sum of benefit expanding public and state-claimed firms in the economy) so every resident advantages from monetary development and advantages from activities that increment proficiency and the capital pay part of the economy (like mechanization).

The significant advantages to a social profit is it lessens reliance upon work pay and gives a supplemental type of revenue for every resident, got from the economy's capital stock. As mechanization increments and work inputs become a more modest part of the economy's bits of feedbacks comparative with capital data sources, and wellsprings of business and work pay evaporate (or descending strain is applied to compensation subsequently prompting stale pay development), declining compensation are counterbalanced by expansions in the social profit payout (for example capital pay). This additionally lessens pay imbalance, and essentially dispenses with abundance disparity (accepting all capital resources are freely claimed and no confidential capital pay exists in the market socialist economy). One more advantage is disposal of the contact between contending work and capital interests that drag down the economy and policy making, since this would really dispense with classes (everybody turns into a section proprietor in the economy).

In a more extensive significance, a "social profit" can take other than an immediate money profit to every resident in an economy. For instance, as China's focal state-claimed endeavors have become more productive and created significant yields, they have been told to move 10% of state-possessed value to support annuity setbacks in the public authority's National Social Security Fund. In this model, state-possessed endeavors give a "social profit" by adding to the benefits for each Chinese resident.

For what reason did financial experts reject Marxism?

To say that financial experts, or rather, standard market analysts reject Marxism, would infer that they have drawn in with Marxism and based on that commitment, have come to dismiss Marxism. However, I would battle that this isn't true with most standard market analysts. Rather than them unequivocally dismissing Marxism in the wake of having made an endeavor to draw in with the works of Marxist financial experts, most standard financial specialists essentially disregard Marxism.

Having expressed that while it is unquestionably a fact that more often than not that standard financial experts overlook Marxism, at times they don't, or rather, they find that occasionally they can't pull off disregarding Marxism, as much they could get a kick out of the chance to. The hour of the Great Depression and the Second World War was one such period. The occasions of that period drove a huge number of individuals, including probably the most conspicuous scholarly people of that time, to scrutinize the suitability and attractiveness of capitalism. It was the occasions of that period that drove standard market analysts to scrutinize their very own portion doctrines, prompting what was known as the "Keynesian unrest" in financial matters. In any case, a few financial specialists of that period went significantly further and started to give old fashioned Karl Marx another once-over, or more probable a first look. One such financial specialist was the British market analyst, Joan Robinson. She was thoroughly prepared in standard financial matters at Cambridge University where she concentrated under A. C. Pigou, who was the understudy and replacement of Alfred Marshall. Also, it was fundamentally Marshallian financial matters that Robinson was prepared for.

From the get-go in her financial matters vocation, she was pushing toward the limits of standard financial aspects, for example, when she thought of her book The Economics of Imperfect Competition. She fostered an examination of how oligopolies work and she began another term, monopsony, to mean the purchasers' adaptation of restraining infrastructures. In this manner, on the off chance that the economy of a nearby local area has only one significant manager, the work market locally can be supposed to be monopsonistic, since that business can set compensation underneath where they would be assuming there were numerous businesses locally. Robinson utilized her examination of monopsony to make sense of how bosses can pull off paying female laborers not exactly male specialists of equivalent efficiency. Later on, Robinson turned into a partner and friend of John Maynard Keynes and was a main explainer of his thoughts concerning macroeconomics. Subsequent to being provoked by Michal Kalecki she started to handle works by Karl Marx, whose work she came to accept expected to get more noteworthy consideration from scholastic financial analysts. That prompted her keeping in touch with her 1942 book An Essay On Marxian Economics. In that book, she would in general stress the likenesses that she saw between Marx's monetary thoughts and those of Keynes, while dismissing Mark's work hypothesis of significant worth. Later on that book was reprimanded by a few Marxist financial specialists like Ernest Mandel who contended that her book shared a portion of the very shortcomings that he saw in crafted by Rosa Luxemburg. In any case, around then, her book went quite far to advance Marx as a figure that standard financial specialists would need to truly take.

In any case, soon after the Second World War, most standard business analysts continued their custom of overlooking Marx. All things considered, that war was trailed by the best period of prosperity throughout the entire existence of capitalism. Simultaneously, the capitalist West was secured in unpleasant philosophical contest with the Soviet Union and different nations of the socialist alliance. The social distress of the 1960's changed things a piece. The ascent of a New Left during that decade tested the philosophical authority of the decision class, and inside the financial matters calling itself, new ways of thinking outside the neoclassical standard started to seem which drew upon heterodox viewpoints, both Marxist and non-Marxist. Furthermore, in the next ten years, capitalist economies would be hit with another monetary emergency, which was described by what came to be called stagflation - that is a blend of downturn and expansion. Yet again some standard financial analysts started to focus harder on those crafted by Marx. Be that as it may, this second would endure just for a brief time. By the mid 1980's, there was a sharp political shift to one side, the economy had started to improve once more, and with these political and financial changes, by and by, standard financial experts started to feel that they could securely overlook Marx's work. And afterward in the 1990's came the fall of the Soviet Union and the socialist alliance in eastern Europe.

For what reason in all actuality do certain individuals say that socialism is equitable?

If going by the meaning of "a vote-based system" signifying "in light of a legitimate concern for the populace/society/local area", then friendly responsibility for a method for creation should be visible as "majority rule possession" of the method for creation. Since the economy works to boost the whole society, a socialist economy can be contended to be fair.

A few socialists will go considerably further and specify that genuine socialism requires not just friendly responsibility for the method of creation, but direct laborers' control of working environments, firms, and organizations. This infers popularity-based administration of all associations and thus the economy overall. This type of socialism is surely intrinsically "popularity based" - yet not all types of socialism element or call for direct laborer's administration (or worker the board) of every association or firm.

Whether socialism is innate "popularity based" or not decisively relies upon what meaning of "a majority rule government" you use. I would contend there isn't anything intrinsically equitable about socialism or capitalism as frameworks of monetary association, except if we stretch the significance of a vote-based system to imply "in light of a legitimate concern for the greater part just". I have additionally heard contentions that simply "unrestricted economies" are just because they conform to address the issues of the greater part (accepting everybody has buying power); this contention fizzles for a similar explanation. If "a vote-based system" basically implies some dubious idea of helping the greater part (rather than alluding to a particular dynamic cycle and administration component), then an absolutist despot who acts in light of a legitimate concern for the larger part would be "basically equitable". This model ought to feature the issue with reasonable extension.

There isn't anything innately more equitable about socialism than capitalism, except if we are discussing a particular variation of socialism where the majority rule direction is dominating in firms all through the whole economy

Was Max Weber a socialist?

No, Max Weber was not a socialist.

Alongside Ludwig von Mises, he was one of the initiators of the socialist calculation against the chance of socialist monetary preparation. Also, he broadly contended that the execution of socialism would essentially build up the "iron enclosure of organization" that he saw as detaining the present-day man.

Then again, his encounters in the Great War moved him somewhat to one side. During the conflict, he turned out to be entirely baffled by the government, which he recently upheld. After the conflict, he was a big fan of the Weimar Republic and was an established individual from the German Democratic Party, which was a left-liberal ideological group, which aligned itself with the SPD.

Have liberals been fooled into character legislative issues instead of Occupy Wall Street and other genuine changes?

If this gets acknowledged, I might want to say this point is extremely obstinate.

Indeed.

Frankly. This is my closely held individual belief. Character governmental issues are inconceivably inept, and an immense exercise in futility. What's more, it irritates me that the left is so enthused about it.

I for one accept wealth dissimilarity to be the greatest divider of I assume .. equity.

Since when we take a gander at what character governmental issues plan to do, it makes gatherings care more about whether any verifiable point of reference has impacted them, as opposed to perceiving the framework that puts that position.

I'm not saying you can't be gay and battle for gay privileges, I am an Omnisexual Cis gendered Korean man. Yet, notice how god damn separating that is. Omnisexual Cis Gendered Korean Man. I'd lean toward you let me know what social class you're in. An individual of color with a billion bucks has TEN FOLD more honor than a solitary white mother living in a trailer park.

As an individual from gen z, I'd say my age is the most inspired by personality legislative issues. Over whatever social financial yakking yak. Furthermore, that is the issue, it's kind of what monstrous partnerships need. Less concentration and consideration regarding the ruin that our ongoing capitalistic framework is in.

I will be straight to the point. You can ask any teen or 20-something about what pronouns are, what sexuality they are, what orientation they are. And so on. Be that as it may, it would be challenging for them to completely make sense of socialism, capitalism, and so on.

What is common humanists' take of agnosticism?

I believe that the response to that question relies on one method, the term agnosticism. If it implies just faith in nothing, that would be something that declared mainstream humanists would dismiss. Then again, this term has had at different times different implications, some of which could be embraced by mainstream humanists.

Hence the term Nihilism in mid-nineteenth century Russia implied something a piece not quite the same as what we mean by the term these days. The Russian Nihilists of the mid-nineteenth century were assailant realists and positivists, who advanced science and reason while dismissing strict notions and political absolutism. The term, Nihilist, in that sense was advocated in Russia by the writer, Ivan Turgenev, in his popular novel, Fathers and Sons, whose primary hero, Bazarov, was introduced as the prototypical Nihilist.

BTW a significant number of the explanations that Bazarov makes in Turgenev's novel were lifted nearly in the same words from publications that Turgenev's past companion, Nikolai Chernyshevsky, had distributed in the magazine, The Contemporary, which Turgenev some of the time composed for as well. Chernychevsky, who was then a significant essayist and manager, was the writer of the novel, What is to be Done? which notwithstanding the way that it was panned by most pundits, impacted a few ages of Russian progressives including the youthful Lenin who acquired the original's title for a popular political parcel of his own.

The ubiquity of Nihilism among Russia's scholarly youth during the mid-nineteenth century both fascinated (and now and again horrified) Russia's best authors of the time. Turgenev committed his clever Fathers and Sons to this issue, while Nihilism figured in a few of Dostoyevsky's books including Crime and Punishment, Notes from the Underground, The Brothers Karamazov, and The Possessed.

At last, Nihilism, by promoting the thoughts of such materialistic and positivist masterminds from the West like Feuerbach, Comte, Darwin, and J.S. Factory, opened the entryway for the later presentation of such conventions as Marxism and disorder which eventually significantly affected Russian legislative issues. Chernychevsky himself was a socialist and is viewed as the dad of progressive socialism in Russia. Karl Marx, for example, had an exceptionally high assessment of himself. As an adversary of the Russian dictatorship, he was ultimately condemned to jail by the Czarist system and later was delivered in broken well-being to live far away, banished for good in Siberia.

For those of you who view yourselves as Socialists however not Communists, would it be that causes you to decide not to distinguish as Communists?

I view myself as both because I would uphold a worldwide Communist framework, yet as a general rule, I comprehend that a framework like that is close to unimaginable after the Cold War and the Red Scare. That is the huge distinction between Socialists and Communists. Socialists would endeavor towards a genuine Marxist world however much as could be expected. Socialists, be that as it may, would attempt to shape a financial and political philosophy around the principal characteristics of Marx's proclamation, and would energize a change towards Marxist, yet wouldn't take a stab at it the same way a Communist would.

For instance, if I somehow managed to compose my proclamation, I would put together it concerning Socialist goals that would have the option to move into a Communist world without any problem. It would support Marxism, yet would set up a general public and government that would work in the split world among Capitalism and Socialism that we have. A ton of Socialist pioneers, like Tito, Mao, Castro, and Lenin, thought or think likewise. One thing to note is that one can't be a Communist without being a Socialist, however, one can be a Socialist without being a Communist. Trust my response is an assistance to you.

Socialism/Social Democracy is a monetary framework, but on the other hand, it's a layout for development. A country that acknowledges Socialism will in general be more philanthropic, better taught, better, centered around the bigger local area, and evenhanded in the treatment of every one of its residents. It is a majority rule.

In any case, it isn't idealistic. Socialism isn't millenarian. As a monetary framework, it doesn't set a definitive appearance of the new Communist man. It doesn't imagine that the State will ultimately shrivel away. It doesn't give the definitive importance of life. It has no assessment of the presence of God. It doesn't try to subvert custom, except for where that custom is a drawback to the local area in general. There are. for instance, parliamentary governments in a few social-majority rule countries. Socialism, OTOH, is idealistic. It holds to a progressive regulation that requires definitive destruction of the old request to construct a Communist society. An outrageous illustration of this is the Khmer Rouge's endeavor to reshape Cambodia through butchering. The greater part of the nations that took on the Soviet or Chinese forms of Communism kept political detainees. A significant number of them were executed as counter-progressives. Socialism capabilities like an assailant religious government, but without God.

Is socialism great? I have perused that in a socialist society, everybody is equivalent and there aren't classes in the public eye. Assuming this is the case, for what reason does dislike it? For what reason are socialists disliked?

Provided that this is true, for what reason does one dislike it?

A great many people have an unfortunate comprehension of socialism, chiefly because Western lawmakers and the media deliberately lie about its significance to befuddle and unnerve their populaces for political help and international strategy objectives. Generally, this was to a great extent driven by personal financial matters and the well-off, which would lose their power and their capabilities completely in a completely socialist framework; however, defenders of socialism and socialism are somewhat to fault particularly after the finish of the Cold War, as they have frequently been poor representatives for these frameworks. Social traditionalists are additionally to a fault, as they are driven by dread of groundbreaking thoughts and change, and will generally connect curiosity and change with detestable tricks.

"For what reason do socialists dislike this?"

There are no "socialist nations" nor has socialism at any point been laid out. The nations individuals frequently allude to as "socialist" (the previous USSR, PRC, et al.) never called themselves socialist nor did they at any point guarantee to have socialist frameworks set up. This mark was given to them by hostile socialist government officials and the media in the Western world. The vast majority of these nations depict themselves as socialist states and professed to be currently constructing a socialist economy. This ought to be clear given a large number of the authority names incorporate "socialist" instead of "socialist" (for example Association of Soviet Socialist Republics, SocialistRepublic of Vietnam, and the Socialist Federal Republic of Yugoslavia).

I have perused that in a socialist society, everybody is equivalent and there aren't classes in the public eye.

Socialism isn't about conceptual fairness, that is an enemy of socialist misrepresentation. Socialism is characterized by normal responsibility for resources and post-work, which suggests tastelessness. "Class" here explicitly alludes to the detachment of individuals into proprietors and laborers - with the normal responsibility for resources, everybody turns into a section proprietor of the economy's useful resources so these differentiations fail to be significant. This is what the "fairness" of socialism and socialism implies.

Is Socialism great

A Marxist could never contend that socialism is "great" fundamentally, yet that it is the consistent result of innovative advancement. Socialism differentiates a phase of human improvement where obligatory work is not generally needed and hence no longer characterizes an individual's presence, liberating them to zero in on higher pursuits and side interests. The material circumstances that led to industrialist connections would never again exist as most work would be profoundly mechanized and most labor and products conveyed openly.

Open-source and unreservedly disseminated programming improvement fills in as a see of a socialist economy: nobody claims the source code and undertakings, everybody is allowed to add to their improvement as they see fit, and everybody approaches the results for nothing. There can be no essential of the optional market for the results since they are bountiful. Regardless of whether this is great depends on you to choose; a Marxist doesn't advocate for socialism or socialism given emotional worth decisions however sees them as regular outgrowths of mechanical improvement reshaping human social association

Does socialism's "control of method for creation" imply that we couldn't have organizations like Google, Tesla, and Facebook, however (1) State Company for Internet Search (2) State Company for Electric Vehicles (3) State Company of Social Media?

It truly relies upon the type of socialism, as there are many structures "public proprietorship" and "social possession" can take. Socialism signifies a scope of speculative frameworks given the transcendence of social responsibility for a method of creation. Customarily, this implied that organizations as such wouldn't exist as free substances; the foundations that involve the economy would be incorporated and enhanced as a solitary element.

That being said, state proprietorship can appear as state-possessed syndications. It can likewise appear as different, contending state-claimed or greater part state-possessed organizations. Google, Tesla, Facebook, et al. might keep on existing as discrete and particular firms with the state taking greater part stakes in them to gather their benefits to transmit to general society at large. There have even been market socialist propositions where the state practices pay privileges as an investor yet needs control (for example the executive's freedoms) over the organizations it possesses, which would protect the autonomy of firms and the liberal market request.

The importance of "social responsibility for a method for creating" or "social control of the method for creation" is the social (vast) allotment of the economy's aggregate delivered abundance (for example property and capital pay). The thought here is to guarantee that always expanding efficiency gains from capital data sources (like robotization) benefit the whole populace as higher salaries and dynamically more limited work shifts. With mechanical advancement comes an extension of dispensable spare energy, which is the valid "domain of opportunity" for socialists. This is the substance of socialism.

Individuals need to quit considering socialism, one particular financial framework that was characterized sometime in the past. There's loads of imagination to be had in envisioning how a cutting-edge socialist economy, receptive to both contemporary mechanical and international real factors, could be coordinated.

Put There are two things individuals mean when they say socialism. Either the Government arrangement of the USSR which I believe is strategically and morally terrible or the exemplary meaning of a stateless, boorish destitute framework which I don't know of the plausibility of.

The monetary constraints of the past never again exist, we should simply control the dissemination of abundance as indicated by the necessities of the people of the common laborers. Fulfill the needs without harming the climate by involving modern Hemp items first of all! Capitalisme is just about extricating abundance to fulfill a bookkeeping fiction. Socialism is just about battling Capitalism, Socialism is tied to withholding the unfortunate back from being excessively poor to more readily safeguard the rich from road brutality. So what is it that this world needs

Are China's state-claimed organizations beneficial? Furthermore, assuming this is the case, what are they doing other than other state-possessed organizations from unfamiliar nations that have in any case fizzled?

Starting around 2022, China's focal state-possessed undertakings (SOEs) are exceptionally productive following quite a while of change. They are more useful concerning complete variable efficiency and limit with regards to development than their confidential area partners.

One significant change China made through SASAC (the State-possessed Assets Supervision and Administration Commission) is changing from resource the board to capital administration. SASAC can zero in on stripping unbeneficial firms and putting capital into beneficial firms to try not to finance unfruitful firms. Most SOEs are presently really blended possession endeavors where the state is the prevailing or significant investor; similarly, numerous confidential firms truly have some state and freely claimed shares too. The subsequent significant change China made is isolating SOEs into absolutely business and public specialist co-ops; the previous amplify their benefits, while the last option will frequently forfeit benefits to accomplishing public assistance objectives (like giving web or cellphone inclusion to unrewarding and generally under-served regions). SOEs likewise went through a progression of administrative change that without a doubt helped support productivity.

Focal SOEs are likewise upgraded and expanded in all to accomplish quicker general development of the whole arrangement of SOEs (and likewise the whole economy) to the detriment of a solitary SOE's transient productivity. This is a drawn-out way to deal with speculation, where apparently misfortune-making adventures like specific rapid rail courses, foundation, and web/5G in specific locales and urban communities might lose transient benefits for the particular firms being referred to, yet will expand the all-out generally speaking efficiency and development of the whole economy over the long haul. For this reason, financial exchange returns have generally been lower in China compared with monetary development contrasted with nations like the United States. It's ideal to consider focal SOEs auxiliaries of one single parent organization (SASAC) that oversees them to increment all out "benefit" of its arrangement of SOEs and the economy in general. So while an individual SOE could give off an impression of being less productive and in this way less proficient all alone, its essential for a more extensive modern methodology to boost returns to the whole economy by taking on different jobs, for example, advancing development and pushing the reception of innovations.

I anticipate the Corporate Social Credit framework and EP/DC (computerized Yuan) - when they are normalized and carried out for an enormous scope - will additionally expand the effectiveness and productivity of Chinese SOEs by smoothing out information accessibility across different associations and making it more challenging for defilement to occur (it's harder for there to be misallocated/"missing assets" when all that data is followed progressively electronically).

The productivity of Chinese SOEs has been expanding beyond a couple of years, and the subject of how to manage state benefits will surely turn into a greater point as China's economy arrives at upper-center and big league salary status. Quickly creating economies reuse their benefits into enterprises that extend their modern base; exceptionally created economies with a more noteworthy size of benefits can utilize them to increment use on friendly spending and merchandise for the whole populace.

Socialism fizzled, and capitalism is so inconsistent and makes destitute individuals distraught. Is the response a social majority rules system or some type of state capitalism like China or Singapore?

Socialism hasn't "fizzled", capitalism doesn't need to be so inconsistent (with regards to paying conveyance) assuming that appropriate public arrangements are executed, social majority rule government in the advanced definition is simply capitalism, and China works on something between state capitalism and market socialism.

For the Western world, a market socialist economy is the following stage forward, along these lines to some portion of what is being created in China: public substances taking stakes in organizations for general society and utilizing the profits to relieve social imbalance by financing social administrations or potentially an essential profit. However, it's easy to refute on the off chance that this is a certified type of "socialism" or on the other hand on the off chance that it's simply capitalism 2.0 (for example state capitalism), one way or the other it is the following coherent move toward the development toward an all the more generally unique socialist financial framework, as it brings useful resources under open proprietorship.

The three fundamental objectives of this game plan ought to be:

1. Promote shared success and dispose of outrageous reliance on wage work or pay rates as a kind of revenue, so the economy can move past the pay work worldview and strategies intended to advance or safeguard occupations (since they are the main type of revenue for most of the populace).

2. Ensure the additions from efficiency development and innovative dislodging of work are gotten back to the whole populace through a social profit/fundamental profit as opposed to compounding imbalance, which likewise increments individual independence and opportunity.

3. Share the weight of work by continuously diminishing the length of the standard week of work to increment extra energy, work on psychological well-being, and keep away from the inefficient propensity to make "horse

crap occupations" or busywork for requiring a check. The customary progressive business/worker dynamic will slowly be dislodged by the inventive economy, and projected much further into the future, progressively by leisure activities accomplished for individual happiness. The mechanical limit concerning a genuine socialist economy where associations are coordinated and enhanced as a solitary element, and likewise, where capital and benefits expansion by sectional firms fails to be the primary engine of financial action and creation, is just being grown now with the rise of data innovation, large information and the modern web. A similarly significant essential that has so far been slippery is the capacity to utilize expanses of information to successfully guide and plan the economy. The expected proficiency and efficiency advantages of a genuine socialist economy will turn out to be more obvious not long from now.

Pay imbalance, which isn't the same thing as abundance disparity, doesn't need to be so terrible under present-day capitalism on the off chance that appropriate relieving social approaches were established. Public endowments or subsidizing for schooling, medical services, and lodging sponsorships for the more extensive working-class affect pay imbalance. They don't determine abundance disparity, or the inconsistent responsibility for producing resources, which market socialism (or a few types of "state capitalism") expects to determine. In any case, these redistributionist strategies are progressively illogical to handle the gigantic measures of imbalance, in pay as well as regarding available energy and independence, created by enormous work dislodging and robotization. There comes where the organization expenses of vigorously burdening and reallocating salaries from progressively beneficial firms to give small advantages to a working-class experiencing stale wages and individuals jobless in light of mechanical joblessness are excessively exorbitant, and it's a good idea to straightforwardly claim and proper wellsprings of capital pay (for example the method for the creation or possibly the value of public firms that own the inexorably robotized method for creation) to help the whole populace. China and Singapore haven't accomplished this (market socialist) stage yet and keeping in mind that comparative on a superficial level, these two nations have a few significant contrasts in the manner they work their state-claimed endeavors. Singapore is an exceptionally changed market economy where the public authority puts resources into its homegrown and worldwide securities exchanges through speculation organizations with the sole objective of boosting returns for its investor, the Ministry of Finance. The incomes to a great extent go to the nation's stores and as of late have been conveyed to assist with financing social administrations somewhat; this is likewise one reason charges are generally low in Singapore. State venture pay isn't utilized to give the more extensive populace a "fundamental profit" or to lessen reliance upon wage work; Singapore is an extremely serious, upsetting, and vocation-driven work market. This isn't the "reply" to every one of the ills of present-day capitalism, yet it gives the seeds to a definitive arrangement as state-possessed shares in the organizations as a way to produce aggregate riches

Bare abuse. Capitalism is tied in with making states of reliance for proprietors to take advantage of, and consistently regresses into control: command throughout one's time, life, and even interests. The last thing a capitalist believes is for people to have independence since not many individuals would intentionally decide to…

Is it off-base to connect socialism with focal preparation? Could it be inappropriate to say focal arranging is "socialistic"?

No, partner socialism with extensive joining and planning isn't erroneous. For sure this is what socialism and social responsibility for a method for creation at first inferred before the expression "focal preparation" were perverted by Austrian school business analysts and liberal disseminators from one viewpoint, and the Soviet coalition on the other. These bastardizations likened "arranging" to something exceptionally thin, unrefined as well as ridiculous.

In its unique detailing, monetary arranging implied the coordination of creation and appropriation so much that the different ventures, divisions, and so forth which contain the useful device of the economy would be streamlined as a solitary element. It was an overall approach to communicating the possibility of a post-capitalist economy, where sectional benefit-boosting firms are presently not the main impetus in the economy.

In the US, on the off chance that moderates call anybody who is certainly not a moderate a "socialist" as certain individuals guarantee, why don't real socialists just emerge and straightforwardly advocate for a socialist monetary framework? What do they need to lose?

I don't think there are an adequate number of real socialists in America right now for there to a major "emerge" occasion, essentially not in that frame of mind of a sizeable piece of individuals who are supportive of making a model of and advancing a socialist financial framework (for example public responsibility for the method for creation, an arranged economy, the finish of compensation work). There are positively some socialist or previously socialist political gatherings and gatherings that draw in help, yet this is centered more around single-issues or explicit strategies under capitalism as opposed to supplanting capitalism with socialism.

For "socialists to emerge", there must be an enormous and semi-coordinated socialist presence in the scholarly world, technical studies and likewise, strategy establishments and research organizations. There must be explicit and substantial strategy propositions for progressing toward socialism and a sizable part of the public stimulated around the likely advantages of pushing toward a socialist economy. This would incorporate a far reaching comprehension of the lack of contemporary work environment association, the breakdown of the law of significant worth, the issue of keeping up with private responsibility for method for delivering riches (particularly in a time of mass robotization) and the possibilities for decreasing the length of the fundamental work day, and maybe a change in mentality where work dislodging via mechanization is seen as a help to human government assistance. As of now this is strange to American governmental issues, and no political figure or association is elevating any methodical option in contrast to capitalism and its foundations.

There are unquestionably individual socialists in varying backgrounds, some of whom aren't even mindful their thoughts and recommendations would fall under the "socialist" name; however they commonly aren't locked

in vigorously in legislative issues and aren't coordinated or even intrigued enough with regards to advancing their thoughts in such a way.
There are little partisan gatherings that portray themselves as "socialist". These are normally little, ancestral gatherings zeroed in either on infighting and political propensities (which isn't interesting to anybody outside their little circle) or on "little potato" social lobbyist causes that don't have anything to do with socialism. The last option surely isn't empowered at the possibility of a socialist economy, in open proprietorship, diminishing the length of the typical business day, or on the expected utility and effectiveness of monetary arranging given present day data innovation. These individuals are not really "socialist" in everything except name, while the partisan gatherings are definitely more keen on ancestral governmental issues and verifiable debates than in socialism itself.

Is market socialism a reasonable long haul plan for "building ('valid') socialism starting from the earliest stage", or is it even more of an "impasse"?

It addresses the following sensible move toward the development of capitalism, particularly when the circumstances that lead to many market foundations are as yet present they actually play a helpful part to play in the asset portion. Moving toward public or aggregate responsibility is a lot less complex than fostering a process for arranging, an elective strategy for bookkeeping (an option in contrast to money related bookkeeping), and substitute goal capabilities for the economy to boost (as an option in contrast to productivity). These last parts will include calculated improvement, prototyping and strategy trial and error before a powerful arrangement is found that can be increased for the whole economy. On the off chance that and when such an answer is found, it ought to normally dislodge markets (for factor inputs in any event) by the ethicality of being more compelling.

A market socialist economy in some structure will be vital on the off chance that embraced by a nation exists in a capitalist world framework and worldwide market system. Assuming a nation were to push toward a monetary framework that boosted some different options from productivity and utilized an alternate bookkeeping framework, and had reasonable authoritative documents that contrasted from the remainder of the world, it would really remove itself (or exceptionally confine itself) from worldwide exchange merchandise and capital. Indeed, even extremely gentle measures of arranging in a market-situated economy, like the contemporary financial framework in the People's Republic of China, is causing grinding with the Western economies (which have liberal market economies). A market socialist economy where market foundations (for example work and capital business sectors, companies, government charges and guidelines) exist yet are to a great extent open or by and large possessed may as yet remain profoundly coordinated with the world economy and advantage from exchange and elevated degrees of

reconciliation, possibly fighting off political struggle and discretionary seclusion from the remainder of the capitalist world.
Likewise potential business sectors in some structure, maybe enhanced by modern strategy arranging, will keep on being essential for quite a while under a socialist economy. Financial change and improvement is a continuous, developmental interaction; there are seldom obvious divisions between various authentic ages. It's similarly as credulous to accept that markets ought to be with no obvious end goal in mind nullified for what it's worth to accept that markets will be for all time the main suitable type of enormous scope asset portion.

Might Jewish individuals at any point be anarcho-capitalists?

The greater part of the establishing masterminds of "Anarchy-capitalism" were of Jewish origin. So clearly, yes.
Is the way of thinking viable with Judaism? Actually no, not actually, yet individuals like Murray Rothbard and Robert Ozick, as well as different masterminds who informed what might turn into "anarchs-capitalist" belief system, for example, Ayn Rand and Herbert von Mines, were agnostics who cared barely at all about Judaism fundamentally.

How might a socialist society progress to a Communist society?

It's amazing nobody has offered a palatable response to this inquiry yet since the response is hard to miss.

Socialism depends on the social responsibility for method for creation, meaning the net working excess has a place with and is appropriated by the whole local area (instead of private proprietors and investors). Socialism depends on socialism, yet at a phase where computerization has advanced so much that prompt work (for example wage work) is not generally needed.

Socialism passes into socialism when the economy's net working excess is adequate to furnish everybody with a respectable and consistently expanding way of life, and the requirement for human work is not generally needed in the economy. The primary focal point of individuals' lives in a socialist society is done working for necessities (for example cash) yet investigating their side interests, interests and relaxation. (One more perspective about this envisioning you'd truly prefer to do in your life in the event that you were rich enough that you didn't need to work). Marx portrayed this as work turning into "life's excellent need" instead of a way to produce a pay.

In the US, on the off chance that moderates call anybody who is certainly not a moderate a "socialist" as certain individuals guarantee, why don't real socialists just emerge and straightforwardly advocate for a socialist monetary framework? What do they need to lose?

I don't think there are an adequate number of real socialists in America right now for there to be a major "emerge" occasion, essentially not in that frame of mind of a sizeable piece of individuals who are supportive of making a model of and advancing a socialist financial framework (for example public responsibility for the method for creation, an arranged economy, the finish of compensation work). There are positively some socialist or previously socialist political gatherings and gatherings that draw in help, yet this is centered more around single issues or explicit strategies under capitalism as opposed to supplanting capitalism with socialism.

For "socialists to emerge", there must be an enormous and semi-coordinated socialist presence in the scholarly world, technical studies, and likewise, strategy establishments and research organizations. There must be explicit and substantial strategy propositions for progressing toward socialism and a sizable part of the public stimulated around the likely advantages of pushing toward a socialist economy. This would incorporate a far-reaching comprehension of the lack of contemporary work environment association, the breakdown of the law of significant worth, the issue of keeping up with private responsibility for the method for delivering riches (particularly in a time of mass robotization), and the possibilities for decreasing the length of the fundamental workday, and maybe a change in mentality where work dislodging via mechanization is seen as a help to human government assistance. As of now, this is strange to American governmental issues, and no political figure or association is elevating any methodical option in contrast to capitalism and its foundations.

There are unquestionably individual socialists in varying backgrounds, some of whom aren't even mindful their thoughts and recommendations would fall under the "socialist" name; however, they commonly aren't locked in vigorously in legislative issues and aren't coordinated or even intrigued enough with regards to advancing their thoughts in such a way. Few partisan gatherings portray themselves as "socialist". These are normally little, ancestral gatherings zeroed in either on infighting and political propensities (which isn't interesting to anybody outside their little circle) or on "little potato" social lobbyist causes that don't have anything to do with socialism. The last option surely isn't empowered at the possibility of a socialist economy, in open proprietorship, diminishing the length of the typical business day, or on the expected utility and effectiveness of monetary arranging given present-day data innovation. These individuals are not really "socialist" in everything except name, while the partisan gatherings are keener on ancestral governmental issues and verifiable debates than on socialism itself.

Is market socialism a reasonable long-haul plan for "building ('valid') socialism starting from the earliest stage", or is it even more of an "impasse"?

It addresses the following sensible move toward the development of capitalism, particularly when the circumstances that lead to many market foundations are as yet present they play a helpful part to play in the asset portion. Moving toward public or aggregate responsibility is a lot less complex than fostering a process for arranging, an elective strategy for bookkeeping (an option in contrast to money-related bookkeeping), and substitute goal capabilities for the economy to boost (as an option in contrast to productivity). These last parts will include calculated improvement, prototyping, and strategy trial and error before a powerful arrangement is found that can be increased for the whole economy. On the off chance that and when such an answer is found, it ought to normally dislodge markets (for factor inputs in any event) by the ethicality of being more compelling.

A market socialist economy in some structure will be vital on the off chance that embraced by a nation exists in a capitalist world framework and worldwide market system. Assuming a nation was to push toward a monetary framework that boosted some different options from productivity and utilized an alternate bookkeeping framework and had reasonable authoritative documents that contrasted with the remainder of the world, it would remove itself (or exceptionally confine itself) from worldwide exchange merchandise and capital. Indeed, even extremely gentle measures of arranging in a market-situated economy, like the contemporary financial framework in the People's Republic of China, are causing grinding with the Western economies (which have liberal market economies). A market socialist economy where market foundations (for example work and capital business sectors, companies, government charges, and guidelines) exist yet are to a great extent open or by and large possessed may as yet remain profoundly coordinated with the world economy and advantage from an exchange and elevated degrees of reconciliation, possibly fighting off the political struggle and discretionary seclusion from the remainder of the capitalist world.

Likewise, potential business sectors in some structures may be enhanced by modern strategy arranging, which will keep on being essential for quite a while under a socialist economy. Financial change and improvement is a continuous, developmental interaction; there are seldom obvious divisions between various authentic ages. It's similarly as credulous to accept that markets ought to be with no obvious end goal in mind nullified for what it's worth to accept that markets will be for all time the main suitable type of enormous scope asset portion.

perspective about this envisioning you'd truly prefer to do in your life if you were rich enough that you didn't need to work). Marx portrayed this as work turning into "life's excellent need" instead of a way to produce pay.

For what reason truly do certain individuals can't stand capitalism?

Since Capitalism is incredibly effective and very imperfect. It's planned around endlessly making abundance in patterns of development and downturn.
You expect the poor to have affluence which is imperfect. Great is that capitalism can increase the expectations of being poor.
Capitalism goes on normal tendencies of mankind to deal with administrations and products. It additionally enjoys the most terrible of humankind with eagerness, control, and cheating.
So the substance of what I am talking about is that Capitalism is defective and can be legitimately censured. However, think about what I say while considering other factors since I am not a financial specialist. They are simply things I've assembled.

Does the way that the most prosperous countries on the planet will generally be capitalist show that capitalism is the best framework and any remaining frameworks ought to be dismissed, or is this not the situation?

Well, you are accepting that the capitalist states don't rebuff non-capitalist states. What's more, you are expecting that the worldwide framework is not a specific worldwide framework that works to the advantage of specific nations. An alternate worldwide framework would help various nations. However, THERE IS ONLY ONE GLOBAL SYSTEM.

However, indeed, to a degree, it shows that capitalism has not yet completely developed and is as yet the best framework to have. Once more, be that as it may, the examination ought not to be between nations since it is manipulated against different nations. You can gauge it being the best country by contrasting it with itself through time. So after you characterize success you can then look at the factors important to gauge it. If success declines, notwithstanding regular causes or wars, you have a valid justification to accept that the capitalist framework has run its full course.

For what reason doesn't socialism work by and by, however capitalism flourishes in numerous nations?

A free undertaking is an unassuming comprehension that remedied the false notion behind mercantilism that abundance was the reason for major areas of strength for a. Adam Smith and Jean-Baptiste Say exhibited that, no, efficiency produces solid economies, including noninflationary riches. You don't have a succeeding economy until individuals have a rising collection of further developing labor and products to buy along with expanding capacity to manage their costs.

Given the roaring abundance created by free endeavor beginning from the late eighteenth 100 years, Karl Marx got on track to catch that "lightning in a container" to all the more enormously work on the parcel of working men by taking out "inactive men with inactive cash." He reasoned that it was the laborers alone who gave worth to items. This belief was obliterated under a full age later by three separate individuals from the Marginalize School of financial matters with their distributed verifications of the Water-Diamond Paradox. Essentially, Marx's case was misleading; it didn't start to address every one of the parts of an item's worth.

A large part of the worth came from the vision of those "inactive men" and their readiness to put their "inactive cash" in danger (making it useful and not inactive by any means).

Deception is one more approach to saying "doesn't work; can't work." Free endeavor takes care of business. The difficulty is that since Marx began tossing around his "hypotheses," the political class all over the planet turned out to be significantly more exceptionally sensitive to cash tricks. Socialism bombed through and through for the absence of free venture, yet a friendly vote-based system and autocracy both allowed free endeavor under political control. As such, the political class became parasitic on free endeavor's capacity to create abundance. Any place where there is a serious level of political control of the economy, free ventures won't fill in too as it could.

At the end of the day, free undertaking (which Marx marked capitalism to make it a philosophical bogeyman) possibly works ideally when free. There is an explanation that a word is essential for the name. Besides, individuals should try to understand that more risky issues like cash, expansion, obligation, downturns, etc are not issues of free undertaking but rather of the more extensive economy.

Who is somebody who experienced childhood in a group of socialist scholastics and became perhaps the present best capitalist?

Casual, I can't imagine any enormous capitalists who emerged from groups of socialist scholastics, although there are likely a couple. I can imagine a few capitalists who are the relatives of driving Communists. Armand Hammer, who was an industry mogul who possessed and controlled a few major organizations, including most quite Occidental Petroleum, was the child of Julius Hammer. Julius was a left-wing extremist and financial specialist, who had been an individual from the Socialist Labor Party and was later an establishing individual from the Communist Party, USA. As things ended up, this family foundation would demonstrate gainful to Armand's business exercises. Not long after the October Revolution in Russia, Armand Hammer had the option to lay out a relationship with Lenin, and during the time of the NEP (New Economic Policy), he had the option to lay out financial matters in the Soviet Union. From that point forward, he stayed dynamic as an unfamiliar financial backer in the Soviet Union, and he knew each top Soviet pioneer from Lenin to Gorbachev. Strategically, Armand Hammer, in contrast to his dad, was no radical, however, was a functioning Republican. He was a major area of strength for Richard Nixon.

Another capitalist, who came from a left-wing family foundation is the mutual funds' director Bill Browder. He is the CEO and fellow benefactor of Hermitage Capital Management. Charge Browder is the grandson of Earl Browder, who was the overall secretary of the Communist Party, USA during the 1930s and the principal half of the 1940s. At one time, Bill Browder was the main unfamiliar financial backer in Russia, yet he in the end got into an extremely severe fight with Putin., which prompted his possible extradition from Russia.

Who is somebody who experienced childhood in a group of socialist scholastics and became perhaps the present best capitalist?

Casual, I can't imagine any huge capitalists who emerged from groups of socialist scholastics, although there are most likely a couple. I can imagine a few capitalists who are the relatives of driving Communists. Armand Hammer, who was an industry mogul who possessed and controlled a few major organizations, including most quite Occidental Petroleum, was the child of Julius Hammer. Julius was a left-wing extremist and money manager, who had been an individual from the Socialist Labor Party and was later an establishing individual from the Communist Party, USA. As things ended up, this family foundation would demonstrate an advantage to Armand's business exercises. Not long after the October Revolution in Russia, Armand Hammer had the option to lay out a relationship with Lenin, and during the time of the NEP (New Economic Policy), he had the option to lay out financial matters in the Soviet Union. From that point forward, he stayed dynamic as an unfamiliar financial backer in the Soviet Union, and he knew each top Soviet pioneer from Lenin to Gorbachev. Strategically, Armand Hammer, in contrast to his dad, was no liberal, yet was a functioning Republican. He was the area of strength for Richard Nixon.

Another capitalist, who came from a left-wing family foundation is the mutual funds chief Bill Browder. He is the CEO and prime supporter of Hermitage Capital Management. Charge Browder is the grandson of Earl Browder, who was the overall secretary of the Communist Party, USA during the 1930s and the main portion of the 1940s. At one time, Bill Browder was the main unfamiliar financial backer in Russia, however, he, at last, got into an extremely harsh quarrel with Putin., which prompted his possible removal from Russia.

How is trader capitalism not the same as modern capitalism?

Vendors trade, they don't deliver. Vendor capitalism depends on benefitting from purchasing a wear at a low cost and selling at a high one.
Modern capitalism, then again, depends on creation. Proprietors of the method for creation (plants, mines, and so on) benefit by charging costs to purchasers that are more noteworthy than the expenses of creation and gathering the overabundance of cash as benefit.

Did Karl Marx at any point recognize the positive parts of capitalism? Assuming this is the case, what explicitly?

Marx was himself guzzled in Hegelism and Positivism, and would in general think history had a kind of moderate nature. He saw capitalism as one of the phases of this advancement, that went from crude socialism to the period of subjugation, to the time of capitalism, and would fundamentally end with the victory of logical socialism. In this sense, he believed Capitalism to be the second most developed phase of human social development and valued Capitalism as a step in the right direction from the past situation because of servitude, and an important stage in the development of socialism. Without a doubt, Capitalism was irreplaceable to the improvement of Scientific Socialism since it gave rise to the lowly class.

For what reason doesn't capitalism appear to be working by raising the wages of transporters enough to let the lack free from accessible drivers?

Capitalism isn't about paying. It is beneficial over all the other things. The lower the rate extremely rich people claim organizations pay, the more benefit they pocket. The shipping framework is set up where the driver is the most noteworthy gamble least awarded gear-tooth in the framework. This is where the "edge" in "overall revenue" is found. If expansion were something genuine in regards to the store network. Furthermore, if it were at 10%, could it not appear to be legit that all in the production network got 10% more in pay to stay aware of all that encompasses them in cost to proceed?

It doesn't. It didn't. It will not work out.

Why is stuff improved in capitalist nations?

More well-off countries will generally have talented and high-level businesses created on the improvement side, and assembling side. On the off chance that they are missing one then they can't have practical experience in it. Stream and plane motor making require high-level and talented assembling and high-level turn of events. They worked in unambiguous things and turned out to be great at it past others. It's exceptionally hard and long to accomplish this. (Chinese organizations frequently figure out and poach top architects, or search for the supplanting development to hop onto the following wave. EV is the wave to beat Gasoline.) Yachts are made in Poland frequently. Italy and Europe have shoemakers. In Cuba, they roll stories, and there's nothing more to it. Not much industry.

Besides capitalism which has been selling the mantra for a very long time that the undetectable hand of the market controls everything, it just so happens, presently it isn't that way. Do the manuals come up short?

Market "guideline" happens because of one major part of an unrestricted economy: nobody can be constrained to trade anything.

So if I could do without what an organization is selling, if I could do without the disposition of the sales rep, on the off chance that I could do without the variety, assuming I heard talk concerning a security or working circumstances, under any condition whatsoever I don't want to purchase, I don't, and there is nothing the organization can do about it.

Nothing, or at least, aside from change. Work on their functioning circumstances, work on their costs, work on their varieties, whatever, to offer to me what it is I need.

What's more, that is a market guideline, and yes truth be told matters about everything.

Contrast this with the government, where you are constrained by regulation to pay for their administrations regardless of whether you need them, regardless of whether you use them. There is no motivating force whatsoever to offer types of assistance individuals need since there is no contest.

Lysander Spooner made his confidential mail center to contend with the USPS. Better costs, better help, and it was a flourishing business. So how did the government respond?

The government made rivalry unlawful. Lysander Spooner was shut down by regulation since he offered the support individuals needed.

Quick forward 100 years and United Parcel Service does likewise.

Perceiving the USPS legitimate imposing business model is just on alleged "top of the line mail" and not boxes, UPS started contending with the USPS.

This time we were fortunate, and they were not shut down.

Fast forward 50 years, Federal Express is established to demonstrate that solid overnight conveyance can be achieved, something neither USPS or UPS at any point endeavored.

Ok, however, this time the American public was not all that fortunate. The USPS began indicting organizations that utilized FedEx "to an extreme", for disregarding the legitimate imposing business model which the USPS has on supposed "top of the line mail". FedEx needs to establish the least bundle sizes to stay away from arraignment.

Might it be said that you are mature enough to recollect when the Post Office didn't have a "following"? They do now because both FedEx and UPS offered the following and the Post Office needed to add it to contend. Furthermore, if an administration organization that appreciates enormous advantages of tax-exempt status, citizen sponsorship, and numerous others, can be handled by "market guidelines", any simple business can be.

How did capitalism beat socialism/Communism?

I'm not a financial specialist, but rather I'd say it is because capitalism has inherent controls, the "imperceptible hand" that Adam Smith expounded on. An excess of stuff drives costs down. Deficiencies drive costs up. If something will create a gain, there will be someone to sell it (until there's too much, then individuals will quit doing as such). The actual market is self-rectifying. In socialism and socialism, someone needs to choose the amount of what to make and what to sell it for. They are in many cases wrong.
There's likewise presumably something to getting to keep your benefits as a propelling impact to work harder and more intelligently.

Has capitalism perhaps been covertly undermined consistently?

It's not exactly confidential, however....
The investigation of financial aspects shows how socialist arrangements in capitalist economies make each of the issues that socialists today whine about.
In America
The expenses of Healthcare
The significant expense of schooling cost
Low wages
Over militarization of the police
The steady conflicts.
On the off chance that we had lower burdens, those were eventually inconceivable.
The skirmish of the lump, the holocaust, and Mao's mass homicide of 65 million were all straightforwardly brought about by socialists in America.

For what reason do such coWhy is stuff improved in capitalist nations?

More well-off countries will generally have talented and high-level businesses created on the improvement side, and assembling side. On the off chance that they are missing one then they can't have practical experience in it. Stream and plane motor making require high-level and talented assembling and high-level turn of events. They worked in unambiguous things and turned out to be great at it past others. It's exceptionally hard and long to accomplish this. (Chinese organizations frequently figure out and poach top architects, or search for the supplanting development to hop onto the following wave. EV is the wave to beat Gasoline.) Yachts are made in Poland frequently. Italy and Europe have shoemakers. In Cuba, they roll stories, and there's nothing more to it. Not much industry.

Besides capitalism which has been selling the mantra for a very long time that the undetectable hand of the market controls everything, it just so happens, presently it isn't that way. Do the manuals come up short?

Market "guideline" happens because of one major part of an unrestricted economy: nobody can be constrained to trade anything.

So if I could do without what an organization is selling, if I could do without the disposition of the sales rep, on the off chance that I could do without the variety, assuming I heard talk concerning a security or working circumstances, under any condition whatsoever I don't want to purchase, I don't, and there is nothing the organization can do about it.

Nothing, or at least, aside from change. Work on their functioning circumstances, work on their costs, work on their varieties, whatever, to offer to me what it is I need.

What's more, that is a market guideline, and yes truth be told matters about everything.

Contrast this with the government, where you are constrained by regulation to pay for their administrations regardless of whether you need them, regardless of whether you use them. There is no motivating force whatsoever to offer types of assistance individuals need since there is no contest.

Lysander Spooner made his confidential mail center to contend with the USPS. Better costs, better help, and it was a flourishing business. So how did the government respond?

The government made rivalry unlawful. Lysander Spooner was shut down by regulation since he offered the support individuals needed.

Quick forward 100 years and United Parcel Service does likewise.

Perceiving the USPS legitimate imposing business model is just on alleged "top of the line mail" and not boxes, UPS started contending with the USPS.

This time we were fortunate, and they were not shut down.

Fast forward 50 years, Federal Express is established to demonstrate that solid overnight conveyance can be achieved, something neither USPS or UPS at any point endeavored.

Ok, however, this time the American public was not all that fortunate. The USPS began indicting organizations that utilized FedEx "to an extreme", for disregarding the legitimate imposing business model which the USPS has on supposed "top of the line mail". FedEx needs to establish the least bundle sizes to stay away from arraignment.

Might it be said that you are mature enough to recollect when the Post Office didn't have a "following"? They do now because both FedEx and UPS offered the following and the Post Office needed to add it to contend. Furthermore, if an administration organization that appreciates enormous advantages of tax-exempt status, citizen sponsorship, and numerous others, can be handled by "market guidelines", any simple business can be.

For what reason do such countless destitute individuals have confidence in capitalism?

I'll explain to you why. I came to California at 20 years of age with a pre-owned vehicle from Florida and a basic wish to simply not be poor. I examined and worked part-time at a Chinese eatery conveying food. Following a couple of years, I got my business degree from a state college, and from that point, I had the option to find a business line of work. I never again was "poor" when I landed that deals position as I succeeded in deals. After being in corporate deals for quite some time, I went into business with $2000. Which thus developed into an extravagant business. Furthermore, presently, after 20 years, I am in the top 1% and have more than whatever I longed for when I previously came here as a poor, worker understudy. Had it not been for capitalism, I don't figure I might have accomplished what I have. Certain individuals would like you to put stock in equity by beating the unregulated economy down, yet the truth is, the unregulated economy makes abundance

For what reason do such countless destitute individuals have confidence in capitalism?

I'll explain to you why. I came to California at 20 years of age with a trade-in vehicle from Florida and a straightforward wish to simply not be poor. I examined and worked part-time at a Chinese eatery conveying food. Following a couple of years, I got my business degree from a state college, and from that point, I had the option to find a business line of work. I never again was "poor" when I landed that deals position as I succeeded in deals. After being in corporate deals for a long time, I went into business with $2000. Which thus developed into an extravagant business. Furthermore, presently, after 20 years, I am in the top 1% and have more than whatever I longed for when I originally came here as a poor, migrant understudy. Had it not been for capitalism, I don't figure I might have accomplished what I have. Certain individuals would like you to have confidence in correspondence by putting the unregulated economy down, however, the truth is, the unrestricted economy makes abundance

Characterizing socialism as the specialists' responsibility for a method for creation, how is nationalization a type of socialism?

Socialism isn't characterized as "laborers' possession" of the method for creation. This definition arose rather as of late on the web as an endeavor to separate socialism from its relationship with state proprietorship, and is just as oversimplified and reductionist as characterizing socialism as "nationalization".

Socialism is characterized as a framework where the method for creation is possessed by the whole society (by the local area in general), an idea normally called "social proprietorship". By bringing the method for creation under the possession and control of the whole local area, the classifications of "laborer" and "proprietor" stop applying as everybody becomes both a benefactor and proprietor (recipient) of the method for creation and hence a recipient of the economy's networking excess. Referring to a framework as "socialist" on the off chance that it doesn't dispense with, or if nothing else works to kill, reliance where people's presences are characterized by wage (or salaried) work, after all, is troublesome."

One proposed model of social possession - and to be sure the most persevering through structure generally preferred by most socialists - is public proprietorship as openly claimed or state-possessed ventures. Nationalization is one approach to laying out open proprietorship - by bringing previously non-public resources into public possession - rather than making new open undertakings without any preparation.

At most nationalization can be a way to accomplish public responsibility for a method of creation, however, the demonstration isn't socialist without help from anyone else. Socialism would be the outcome of an extensive nationalization program that includes a large portion of the economy to make everybody a section proprietor and recipient of the (presently) openly claimed resources.

Involving nationalization and public proprietorship for socialist closures is to carry the method for creation into the possession and control of a body addressing society as an antecedent to revamping the economy overall and incorporating the method for creation into an arrangement of coordinated monetary preparation. Completely created socialism would be a framework with its framework elements and inward working rationale, particularly from capitalism. On the other hand, public possession can appear as independent state-claimed undertakings working to expand benefits in a market economy, which would be an illustration of market socialism.

In any case, even open possession is just a subset of social proprietorship; there are different recommendations like cooperatives and the hall (however this last idea for the method for creation is more a trait of a high-level socialist society).

Not one or the other "specialist proprietorship" nor "nationalization" characterize socialism: the principal idea is redundant and the subsequent one is all things considered a way to change to state possession, which itself is just a subset of social possession less destitute individuals have confidence in capitalism?

I'll explain to you why. I came to California at 20 years of age with a pre-owned vehicle from Florida and a basic wish to simply not be poor. I examined and worked part-time at a Chinese eatery conveying food. Following a couple of years, I got my business degree from a state college, and from that point, I had the option to find a business line of work. I never again was "poor" when I landed that deals position as I succeeded in deals. After being in corporate deals for quite some time, I went into business with $2000. Which thus developed into an extravagant business. Furthermore, presently, after 20 years, I am in the top 1% and have more than whatever I longed for when I previously came here as a poor, worker understudy. Had it not been for capitalism, I don't figure I might have accomplished what I have. Certain individuals would like you to put stock in equity by beating the unregulated economy down, yet the truth is, the unregulated economy makes abundance

For what reason do such countless destitute individuals have confidence in capitalism?

I'll explain to you why. I came to California at 20 years of age with a trade-in vehicle from Florida and a straightforward wish to simply not be poor. I examined and worked part-time at a Chinese eatery conveying food. Following a couple of years, I got my business degree from a state college, and from that point, I had the option to find a business line of work. I never again was "poor" when I landed that deals position as I succeeded in deals. After being in corporate deals for a long time, I went into business with $2000. Which thus developed into an extravagant business. Furthermore, presently, after 20 years, I am in the top 1% and have more than whatever I longed for when I originally came here as a poor, migrant understudy. Had it not been for capitalism, I don't figure I might have accomplished what I have. Certain individuals would like you to have confidence in correspondence by putting the unregulated economy down, however, the truth is, the unrestricted economy makes abundance

Characterizing socialism as the specialists' responsibility for a method for creation, how is nationalization a type of socialism?

Socialism isn't characterized as "laborers' possession" of the method for creation. This definition arose rather as of late on the web as an endeavor to separate socialism from its relationship with state proprietorship, and is just as oversimplified and reductionist as characterizing socialism as "nationalization".

Socialism is characterized as a framework where the method for creation is possessed by the whole society (by the local area in general), an idea normally called "social proprietorship". By bringing the method for creation under the possession and control of the whole local area, the classifications of "laborer" and "proprietor" stop applying as everybody becomes both a benefactor and proprietor (recipient) of the method for creation and hence a recipient of the economy's networking excess. Referring to a framework as "socialist" on the off chance that it doesn't dispense with, or if nothing else works to kill, reliance where people's presences are characterized by wage (or salaried) work, after all, is troublesome."

One proposed model of social possession - and to be sure the most persevering through structure generally preferred by most socialists - is public proprietorship as openly claimed or state-possessed ventures. Nationalization is one approach to laying out open proprietorship - by bringing previously non-public resources into public possession - rather than making new open undertakings without any preparation.

At most nationalization can be a way to accomplish public responsibility for a method of creation, however, the demonstration isn't socialist without help from anyone else. Socialism would be the outcome of an extensive nationalization program that includes a large portion of the economy to make everybody a section proprietor and recipient of the (presently) openly claimed resources.

Involving nationalization and public proprietorship for socialist closures is to carry the method for creation into the possession and control of a body addressing society as an antecedent to revamping the economy overall and incorporating the method for creation into an arrangement of coordinated monetary preparation. Completely created socialism would be a framework with its framework elements and inward working rationale, particularly from capitalism. On the other hand, public possession can appear as independent state-claimed undertakings working to expand benefits in a market economy, which would be an illustration of market socialism.

In any case, even open possession is just a subset of social proprietorship; there are different recommendations like cooperatives and the hall (however this last idea for the method for creation is more a trait of a high-level socialist society).

Not one or the other "specialist proprietorship" nor "nationalization" characterize socialism: the principal idea is redundant and the subsequent one is all things considered a way to change to state possession, which itself is just a subset of social possession

What's the contrast between socialism and socialism?

The possibility of socialism was exceptionally old and numerous networks shared normal possession ashore, and assets before, however, they were restricted with the degree of work efficiency, surplus items, socio social and material turn of events.

Numerous Religions in the past accepted uniformity, faith as belief in higher powers, and sharing of material prosperity and riches, for the turn of events and government assistance in the more seasoned class social orders. Numerous Religions embraced socialism however they couldn't prevail with regards to bringing socialism, since they wouldn't have the foggiest idea about the main driver of the issue, which was a type of "confidential property" in the method for creation, this causes differences, financial issues and disparities in any class social orders. Capitalism was the most recent period of "social turn of events" which lays out the "confidential property" freedoms on "method for creation", and laws of trade given traditional financial matters. A decision class "super-structure" structures, similar to a religion, as state, legislatures, Banks, regulation framework, police, Bureaucracy, and Military. This hypothesis was proposed by the later Marxist and Leninist socialists.

How do class and "social separations" arise, and what are their underlying drivers? Religions discuss different components of a moral person and noticed specific practices for agreement, opportunity, harmony, individual freedoms, and incomparability of all-powerful over all life. Be that as it may, why do we track down friendly and financial issues in all class social orders which religions mightn't? The job of religion might be to accommodate the separated and socially delineated gatherings, by bringing illusionary solidarity, and maintaining the holiness of private property as one's leafy foods. Presently a day, in capitalism, this was finished by the states.

In antiquated times it was religion and Monarchy, who controlled with the insight of property, however, the general abundance looks acquired by tax assessment from the majority, "administering classes" were accepted to serve the interests surprisingly who go under their standard of realms or domains.

At the point when realms were decentralized, we track down many packages of little networks, towns, and shut frameworks in times past, with possessed riches and property in like manner. This framework we might need to inexact as the middle of the road between socialism and crude communism .

The annihilation of numerous "public possession," seizures, and dispossession of many gatherings and crude networks, from the land, for private property, and improvement of the current foundation frames the premise of present-day capitalism and Urbanization. Cash expects to be an "extraordinary influence" called Capital, which develops the confidential property of gatherings or people as their own made riches, involving the market as an upholding request of every single social relationship. Notwithstanding property, a specialized method for creation creates, which lays out a set of rules and regulations utilizing the state and its decision class, which assists with authorizing the desire of the Capitalist framework. The Religions advanced "Idealistic socialism" and guaranteed great after-life, additionally re-birth of the hindered individuals in the rich and heavenly family. In any case, the advanced thought of Socialism depended on the Scientific hypothesis of Marxism, which accepts the "normal responsibility for a method for creating" by all specialists in the general public, with an endeavor to nullify wage work, market, property honors, and Capital. This would empower the improvement of the social orders to their most significant level by engaging all people.

Why do we need to consider Marxism as logical? It maintains the hypothesis of "social development" as an advancement in the "method for creating" utilized by individuals. At the point when capitalism arrives at the immersion and maximum capacity, the specialized advances would eliminate the shortage and rivalry, or the capitalism was "emergency inclined" bringing about the upheaval in the difference in "property possession" and expanded "socialization of creation". That is to say, Marx's view was that an emergency of capitalism could clear a path for socialism, which adds to the "future turn of events" of the expulsion of shortage and carrying overflow to the whole of humanity. Then we could have a wide range of individuals and laborers, who appreciate great "expectations for everyday comforts". A boorish society doesn't mean an ideal world, however a "government assistance collective". "Government assistance state" was slanderous for Marxists and socialists, since they accept "state" or government, as a "coercive independent establishment" of the Bourgeoisie, who utilize the state and assailants or police to loathe the "working people" and poor people. Numerous Marxists expect to grumble that there exists "division of work" and contest among laborers, assuming they truly need socialism, they need not vie for "little impetuous" tossed by the "classes above" who utilize.

Social Darwinism was an opposite thought and managing class revenue, it was an extreme right philosophy of Capitalism, however, on the center-left and moderate side, Capitalism upholds "Common socialism" as a blend of market and a majority rules system, which goes against one another. Social Darwinism discusses a philosophy of existential emergency for individuals in any coordinated society and civilization. Be that as it may, they consider the weakness of the poverty classes whose populace develops more than the accessibility of the means and assets to support them. Nonetheless, Marx disposed of this thought of shortage as not regular however it was fake, it's a consequence of "class gap" and "class struggle," not the normal peculiarity! A huge number have developed the extent of "social Darwinism" hypothesis like Spencer, Darwin, Malthus, Max Weber, Durkheim, and Adam smith (who spots the market as a social power as an "undetectable hand," yet Marx demonstrated it as a method for capitalists to take advantage of work power). More data could be found in the books and works like this.

The main contrast was "Social Darwinism" conveys a few individual personal circumstances, "collective interests" of delineated bunches like race, language, and ethnic-based interests as well as observing the monetary guidelines of Capitalism. "Common socialism" attempts to lay out a moderate strict philosophy of market and the "confidential property", liberated from the decision class and all inclinations.

In any case, the decision philosophy of the "social majority rules system" was considered as "working class" fascism by the "communist history specialists", where "confidential property", capital, and government assistance tax collection were legitimized.

Marxists view capitalist society as consisting of classes that are isolated on a goal and financial premise, in light of relations of property possessing and privileges on methods for creation. A philosophy of "social majority rules system" addresses the interests of the "property claiming class" even though it was accepted, a reformist government assistance state could work and go to redistributive lengths.

The distinction between "social vote-based system" and "moderate socialism" was dark. Marx was the primary socialist to depict socialism as the normal responsibility for "of creation" and land, where populist socialism might be conceivable by ousting the standard of the Bourgeoisie. He composed an "isolated program" politically for the foundation of "fascism of the working people". It means to safeguard socialism or a change stage, against counter-transformation by Bourgeoisie. It requires the common laborers to catch the political power (this social power was laid out to policing and watching the "capitalist property"). It requires the utilization of protection and furnished uprising or rebellion by the specialists and save armed force against the capitalist state. The Russian unrest made a fervor the foundation of socialism in the west, during a "radical conflict" that occurred in the west (First and second universal conflicts).

With the improvement of division of work among laborers and because of the government, work nobility arose. Consequently, the reformist current of "social majority rules system" and worker's organization, Anarcho-syndicalism arose in the rich western capitalist social orders. Another layer of laborers like Bureaucracy and specialized intellectuals, Bankers, assistants and chiefs, police and military arose, who monitor the capitalist state and safeguard the capitalist supervisors and their property. Propertied classes and financially sound individuals were likewise the "administering class" in many states.

Yet, once more, both of these ideal "Middle-class socialism" with a government assistance state and "Marxian socialism", was not seen by and by, they highlight all deviations, and there might be a re-foundation of Capitalism as the main option for the emergency.

To comprehend Social Darwinism, We need to contrast it with Marxian thought of socialism. Likewise, check these connections which appear to be applicable.

For what reason do the Democrats incline toward the left and Communism/socialism?

This, to be honest, couldn't possibly be more off-base. They favor huge administrative arrangements which develop "top-down" arrangements, blending effectively into capitalist corporate organizations.

Organization catches [Example: The Regulatory Capture of the FDA] by confidential industry goliaths covers what turns into a brought together capitalist and secret government regulatory activity.
Thus, toppling the very republic that made that state administration, supposedly aimed at serving residents' inclinations with it.
Socialism is a modern republic that supersedes through a Constitutional change upheld by the one major modern association, both capitalist and covert government civil servants with the Socialist Industrial Republic, where all delegates are generally associated with coordination of industry, have no characterized term of office, and are dependent upon moment review by their electors.
The majority of the present legislators, without the information on socialism, as a result, grow a corporate (AKA, Fascist) state.

Might you at any point be a socialist yet at the same time a furious protector of the US Republic and Constitution?

Totally!! You can't be a socialist without it! For different reasons, this is socialism: An Industrial Republic!

The way taken by laborers should fabricate a strong power at the voting station, and a strong monetary association to implement the polling form's results.

Danial DeLeon, a fellow benefactor of the IWW, who passed on 1914: "Presently, the backstabber is a weakling. Like a defeatist, he will play the domineering jerk, as we see the capitalist class doing, close to the feeble, the powerless because of disordered, regular workers. Before the solid, the domineering jerk creeps. Allow the political temperature to climb to the reason behind risk, then, all monkeying with the thermometer, in any case, your capitalist will shake in his taken boots; he won't set out to battle; he will escape. Essentially I, for one's purposes, hope to see him escape. However, he will not accept if, back of that polling form that has raised the political temperature to feverish heat, is the cloud of the modern association, in full ownership of the modern foundations of the land, coordinated fundamentally and, thusly, equipped for expecting the lead of the country's creation. The total modern association of the average will then have protected the serene issue of the battle.

"Be that as it may, maybe the capitalist may not escape. Maybe, in the ridiculousness of fury, he might stand up. Such a lot of the more terrible for him. They may suggest that in the modern association of the common laborers of the land, they will be ready to wipe the earth with the defiant usurper quite promptly and shield the right that the voting form announced."

Here we see that Socialist development is a safeguard, not a foe, of the Constitutional Republic as it moves the Republic structure by Constitutional revision from a regional stage, to a modern republic.

In American legislative issues, does the "elephant" address capitalism while the "jackass" addresses socialism?

Half right. The jackass addresses despotism. It tries to freeze class structures with major areas of strength for any of the states engaged with every specialist's life to guarantee a consistent populace.
On the other hand these show bias toward one portion over another specialist gathering to cement divisions among the working people.
In lockstep with every single fundamentalist ancestor and its previous concentration, it requires a racial, and ethnic accentuation, again not laborer solidarity.
Socialism is a modern republic. Socialists advocate the laborer Unionist association along conservative rules that incorporate a prompt review of any delegate chosen, by similar constituents.
It turns into a modern republic resembling and shadowing preceding genuine administration, current confidential modern administration frameworks.
This requests specialist fortitude alongside both comprehension and true regard for the standards of conservative administration.
This would be communicated politically through the support of a Constitutional change providing all capacity to the then republic of industry.
The party upholding that alteration (the party of socialism), breaks down when the State does with the entry of the revision.

Popularity based capitalism

Capitalism depends on the confidential responsibility for a method for creation and circulation. Presently attempt and sort out how there can be a majority rule government when the method for a living are controlled and possessed by a rich minority?

Capitalism gives a similarity to a majority rules government yet when you start to expose what's underneath it looks like a pail of shit. The type of a majority rule government applied in capitalism is delegated a vote-based system where contenders for political office guarantee everything except convey benefits for the meager few.

A majority rule government implies the shortfall of honor, pursuing our choices from a place of correspondence. A vote-based system implies that we should live in an open society with unlimited admittance to the data pertinent to social issues. It implies that we ought to have the ability to follow up on our choices because without such powers choices are pointless. All in all, be it Labor, Liberal, Tory, or rule by whatever other sort of government, how does the activity of the state compare to what socialists contend ought to be a vote-based society?

For socialists, the standard of government can never be popularity based. However, it might incorporate a few coincidental capabilities emerging from the requirements of individuals; the principal work of the state is the running of a class-partitioned society; an arrangement of monetary double-dealing.

In states' employers are a special part of society. They cause the regulations which safeguard the property privileges of a minority who own and control regular assets, industry, production, and transport. These are the methods for life on which we as a whole depend, yet the vast majority of us have nothing to do with how they are utilized. Behind Parliament, legislatures work covertly. They are essential for the division of the world into rival capitalist states. With the back-up of their military, they seek after public capitalist interests. However, the legislators who run it very well might be chosen, the state is something contrary to a majority rules government

Creation is claimed and constrained by organizations, some of them global companies with huge monetary power pursuing the choices on what ought to be delivered for the business sectors available to be purchased at a benefit. Through corporate power they conclude how merchandise ought to be delivered and the circumstances in which work is finished. Once more, this is something contrary to a majority rules system

All in all, how might a majority-rules government be satisfied in socialism?

This requires the nullification of the state and its substitution by an arrangement of majority rule organizations. This can work from a premise of normal possession and creation exclusively for use. Normal proprietorship implies that all individuals all through the world will remain in equivalent relationships with one another. This will be a relationship of all people settling on the choices and co-working to deliver merchandise and sort out networks to their greatest advantage.

The popularity-based association surprisingly as residents of the world would have to work through various sizes of social co-activity. Locally, around our country, we would be engaged with our ward or neighborhood. Indeed, even now, there are a huge number of people all through the country who work deliberately onward and in regional gatherings and around neighborhoods to support their networks. In any case, these endeavors would be extraordinarily upgraded by the opportunities of a general public run totally through deliberate co-activity.

Such a nearby association would be with regards to provincial co-activity which could work by adjusting the designs of present public states. While certain divisions, for example, Inland Revenue and the Treasury, which are crucial for the state would be abrogated, others like Agriculture and the Environment could have a significant task to take care of, particularly in the beginning of socialism. Such designs - adjusted to the requirements of socialist society - could be important for provincial gatherings and would aid crafted by carrying out the choices of territorial populaces.

During the beginning of socialism almost certainly, the association of world co-activity would have to happen through a world gathering. Since the things we want currently are delivered and dispersed through a world design of creation, and because its current capitalist nature has achieved massive issues, activity to tackle them would be expected on a world scale.

For instance, it would be fundamentally important to set up a biologically harmless world energy framework straightaway. Essentially, the endless a great many individuals experiencing yearning and frantic destitution would require a significant expansion in food creation. For this work, the Food and

Agricultural Organization of the UN would finally have the option to utilize its ability and information on world circumstances to assist with taking care of the issues of lack of healthy sustenance. Once more, in the first place, individuals in socialism would confront an immense undertaking in giving each secure and happy lodging. This would call upon the endeavors of networks all through the world, particularly in those locales where a method for creation was advanced. Such world ventures could be coordinated through fitting divisions of a world board.

At the point when we propose various sizes of social co-activity, for example, neighborhood, provincial, and world scales, this isn't an issue of there being a pecking order with power situated at any essential issue.

What we expect is both a coordinated and adaptable arrangement of majority rule association which could be adjusted for an activity to take care of any issue in any of these scales. This essentially considers that issues and the activity to tackle them emerge from nearby issues and this likewise reaches out to the local and world circles.

Critical to the subject of a majority rules system isn't simply the capacity to come to conclusions about what to do yet, in addition, the powers of activity to complete those choices. For a long time, capitalist legislators looking for office have vowed to take care of the lodging issue along with the issues of destitution, joblessness, contamination, wrongdoing, the well-being administration, and some more. They have fizzled because they try to run a framework driven by benefit, which forces serious monetary impediments on what should be possible and which subsequently can't be reasonably controlled. This makes a joke of the possibility of a vote-based system. In any case, with the cancellation of the market framework, networks in socialism can not just arrive at free and popularity-based conclusions about what should be done; they will likewise be allowed to utilize their assets to accomplish those points.

The conciliatory sentiments that we hear pretty much consistently from capitalist lawmakers that they miss the mark on cash assets to take care of issues show how the fetishism of cash has twisted their reasoning. Issues are not settled with cash assets, truth be told. They are settled by individuals utilizing their work, abilities, and vital materials and there is, as a matter of fact, an overflow of these material assets. Yet, it will take the relations of the normal proprietor

Benefits of Capitalism

Capitalism is an economy in light of unregulated economies where assets and firms are exclusive. Practically speaking, this typically includes a state intercession to safeguard private property and control specific parts of the economy. Most would contend that the UK and US are capitalist notwithstanding the public authority spending somewhere in the range of 35 and 40% of GDP.

1. What is the other option?

It might be said something similar for capitalism. Essentially, when states endeavor to control the economy. We end up with issues, for example,
Debasement
Absence of motivations
Unfortunate data

2. Productive Allocation of Resources.

In principle, capitalism or the 'imperceptible hand of the market' guarantees assets are appropriated by shopper inclinations. Firms are not compensated for delivering products individuals don't need.

3. Effective Production.

In a market framework, firms have motivators to be gainfully effective - reducing expenses to further develop seriousness and efficiency. If organizations don't stay useful and effective they will leave the business.

4. Dynamic Efficiency.

This is productivity over the long haul. Firms in a capitalist framework need to answer changes in buyer inclinations and answer new customer patterns.

5. Monetary Incentives.

Proof recommends that individuals work hardest when there is individual monetary motivation. For example business, people just face challenges in setting up organizations on account of the potential for an enormous monetary prize. On the off chance that this extension for private benefit is missing, new firms will not be set up.

6. Imaginative obliteration.

J. Schumpeter contended a strong impact of capitalism was the possibility of 'imaginative obliteration'. On the off chance that organizations become wasteful and obsolete, they leave the business. This prompts transient issues - joblessness. In any case, it permits assets - capital, and work to move to new, more imaginative, and productive businesses.

7. Monetary opportunity helps political opportunity.

To a mastermind like Milton Friedman or Joseph Hayek, a monetary opportunity of capitalism is related to political opportunity. An express that restricts the freedoms of people to set up a business or pick where to work will constantly confront more prominent political obstruction
Be that as it may, after seeing political constraints in places like Chile, Friedman conceded financial opportunity was not adequate to ensure political opportunity, but rather it was a beginning stage.

8. System for conquering segregation and uniting individuals.

Capitalism supports exchange between various countries and various individuals. This monetary motivator attempts to separate boundaries and go past tight partisan contrasts
Gary Becker made a comparable point that the benefits thought process would punish those organizations and people who rehearsed racial segregation.

9. Various sorts of capitalism.

Capitalism has advanced to incorporate parts of the social majority rules system and government intercession. Indeed, even the most 'capitalist social orders' have a level of government mediation - for instance, state arrangement of foundation, schooling, medical care, and benefits. However, notwithstanding government intercession to treat the limits of capitalist disparity, the industry is as yet run along comprehensively unrestricted economy lines.

10. Rising expectations for everyday comforts.

Capitalism has added to rising expectations for everyday comforts and fall in outright neediness. Since China and different nations of south-east Asia turned out to be more 'capitalist and unrestricted economies, their economies have developed prompting an ascent in expectations for everyday comforts and a fall in degrees of destitution.

Advantages of a capitalist economy

Capitalism, as we know, is an economy where assets and firms are exclusive in unregulated economies. Typically, this generally includes an administration intercession to control specific parts of the economy and safeguard private property. A few benefits are incorporated inside a capitalist economy.

1. Streamlining of Resources.

Since government intercession is kept at a restricted level, a few issues that for the most part emerge with government mediation including debasement and unfortunate flow of data inside the market are forestalled, permitting individual motivations to fill in as hard as conceivable to accomplish however much as could reasonably be expected. Additionally, the significant element of capitalism to create a gain pushes for the ideal use of accessible assets. There is extraordinary rivalry among makers to catch a greater lump of the market size, so capitalists are continually watching out for ways of expanding the assets utilized underway to decidedly build their overall revenue in the opposition.

2. Prompts expanded individual abundance.

As the capitalist economy is reliant upon the push variable of people, there is no restriction to the degree of abundance an individual can gather through movement inside the economy.
As organization capability improves so does the capacity for individuals to travel through the friendly class as an expansion in abundance is accessible. This pushes people to work harder in light of a legitimate concern for self-safeguarding to accomplish more. Benefit increment inside the economy and individual industry, permits development in riches and company assets, assets that will be utilized to best help the organization and thus the economy by advancing unfamiliar ventures.

3. Increments buyer decisions.

Capitalism permits people to pick both items to buy and work potential open doors. It permits assets to be disseminated by purchaser decision raising the market in a more useful buyer well-disposed range.

People have an opportunity to decide to buy and take part in essentially all monetary exercises with little limitation. Advancing exchange among countries and people commonly benefits people and the actual economy.

4. More effective creation

Through capitalism, firms and organizations are learned to deliver with more noteworthy proficiency, by reducing expenses and further developing productivity.

This is finished with a means to forestall misfortunes in an industry where the contest is high, bettering the economy all in all.

In various businesses, organizations successfully answer changes in buyer wants. In endeavors to guarantee the most elevated conceivable degree of efficiency, monetary motivations are given to workers by organizations to all the more likely work on personal responsibility in organizational capability. This is useful on a worldwide level as nations rehearsing capitalism by and large become commendable imaginative fronts for development in innovation and ramifications of useful changes.

5. Brings about benefit augmentation

Benefit boost is a primary need inside the capitalist state.

This can be created by gathering shopper needs. This causes huge providers of labor and products that are comparative and expand in brands to consider client differentiation and distinction.

There is rivalry among makers to catch a greater lump of the market size, so capitalists are generally keeping watch for ways of boosting the assets utilized underway to decidedly build their net revenue and potentially beat the opposition.

Capitalism likewise enjoys a few benefits which are as per the following:

An economy is the riches and assets that are accessible in a particular locale or nation given the degrees of creation or utilization of required labor and products. There are two distinct kinds of economic choices that can advance capitalism: formal and casual.

The conventional economy comprises a market driven by the public authority or neighborhood powers that keep explicit guidelines or guidelines that apply to everybody. Casual economies exist with no proper policies that organizations or clients should follow to have their necessities met. Capitalism is a type of a proper economy. Organizations should work inside the laid out limits, observing guidelines and arrangements, to remain consistent with the assumptions of the public authority. Rather than controlling the economy using a focal arranging authority like the range of socialism-based economies, capitalism centers around development, decision, and opportunity. These advantages come to the detriment of the more prominent social government assistance.

The focal point of the monetary exercises in capitalism is to make a benefit. These are the benefits and weaknesses to consider from that point of view.

Merits of Capitalist System

1. Capitalism gives buyers choices.

Under the construction of capitalism, purchasers get to pick what they need to consume. It is through the accessibility of decisions that the opposition creates in the confidential area to give the most ideal labor and products. This benefit prompts more significant levels of advancement because the regular individual will purchase the most ideal thing that they can manage. You will for the most part see reasonable things of better quality under this monetary construction than you would in a socialist economy.

2. There is more noteworthy effectiveness to economics.

Capitalism centers around labor and products that are delivered given how many customer requests exist for the thing. This benefit permits an organization to reduce expenses since they realize what is required, at a particular quality, and in light of a specific stock number. It makes a capacity to find new motivators that can reduce expenses oso that cost is a cutthroat consideration in the brain of a customer. Certain individuals can pick extravagant things, while others can settle on a passage-level item. One way or another, the necessities of every individual are met - staying away from the waste that can happen in different frameworks.

3. Financial development happens with capitalism.

The GDP increases when capitalism is available in the economy since advancement prompts more appeal, which then, at that point, prompts serious buying. At the point when a purchaser's life is better as a result of the items or administrations they've bought, then, at that point, there is a choice to work on their way of life after some time. A confidential undertaking can utilize monetary assets more effectively than the public area, and that implies the benefits can go right once again into the situation to help everybody during every c

Conclusion

The world over the times has acknowledged the up-sides of truth if these belief systems and ignored the negatives. Presently, none of the economies on the planet decides to relate to any of these belief systems rigorously.

Government assistance is the normal and irrefutable worry of all regardless of whether they remember to continue to clear a path for the singular measurement and advance the development and legitimate gathering.

Further, empathetic capitalism and corporate social obligation are new standards joining these two very inverse philosophies for smooth and secure execution of the economy for the populace.